How You Can Be Led
By The Spirit Of God

BOOKS BY KENNETH E. HAGIN

His Name Shall Be Called Wonderful
Paul's Revelation: The Gospel of Reconciliation
How To Walk in Love
New Thresholds of Faith
Prevailing Prayer to Peace
Concerning Spiritual Gifts
Bible Faith Study Course
Bible Prayer Study Course
The Holy Spirit and His Gifts
*The Ministry Gifts (Study Guide)
Seven Things You Should Know About Divine Healing
El Shaddai
Zoe: The God-Kind of Life
A Commonsense Guide to Fasting
Must Christians Suffer?
The Woman Question
How You Can Be Led by the Spirit of God
What To Do When Faith Seems Weak and Victory Lost
The Name of Jesus
The Art of Intercession
Growing Up, Spiritually
Bodily Healing and the Atonement
Exceedingly Growing Faith
Understanding the Anointing
I Believe in Visions

BOOKS BY KENNETH HAGIN JR.

*Man's Impossibility — God's Possibility
Because of Jesus
The Key to the Supernatural
*Faith Worketh by Love
Blueprint for Building Strong Faith
*Seven Hindrances to Healing
*The Past Tense of God's Word
Healing: A Forever-Settled Subject
How To Make the Dream God Gave You Come True
Faith Takes Back What the Devil's Stolen
"The Prison Door Is Open — What Are You Still Doing Inside?"
Itching Ears
Where Do We Go From Here?
How To Be a Success in Life
Get Acquainted With God
Showdown With the Devil
Unforgiveness
The Answer for Oppression

*These titles are also available in Spanish. Information about other foreign translations of several of the above titles (i.e., Dutch, Finnish, French, German, Indonesian, Polish, Russian, Swahili, and Swedish) may be obtained by writing to: Kenneth Hagin Ministries, P.O. Box 50126, Tulsa, Oklahoma 74150.

How You Can Be Led By The Spirit Of God

Kenneth E. Hagin

Unless otherwise indicated, all Scripture quotations in this volume are from the *King James Version* of the Bible.

Fifth Printing 1984

ISBN 0-89276-500-3

In the U.S. write:
Kenneth Hagin Ministries
P.O. Box 50126
Tulsa, Oklahoma 74150

In Canada write:
Kenneth Hagin Ministries
P.O. Box 335
Islington (Toronto), Ontario
Canada, M9A 4X3

Contents

Preface

God has been talking to me recently about something I failed to do.

Twenty years ago, in February of 1959 in El Paso, Texas, the Lord appeared to me in a vision. He came into my room at 6:30 in the afternoon, sat down in a chair by my bedside, and talked with me for an hour and a half. I tell more about this in the book, but I want to emphasize something here first.

He talked to me about the ministry of the prophet (Eph. 4:11,12). Then He said, "I did not put prophets in the Church to guide the New Testament Church. My Word says, 'As many as are led by the Spirit of God, they are the sons of God.' Now if you will listen to me, I am going to teach you how to follow my Spirit. Then, I want you to teach my people how to be led of the Spirit."

I am ashamed that I have let twenty years go by without teaching too much along this line. Occasionally I would get into the edge of it, but I did not really teach on it.

So, in recent times, the Lord has stirred me up and I am beginning to teach more in this area. This book is a part of that stirring.

1

The Lamp of the Lord

"For as many as are led by the Spirit of God, they are the sons of God." —Romans 8:14

"The Spirit itself (Himself) *beareth witness with our spirit, that we are the children of God."*—Romans 8:16

"The spirit of man is the candle of the Lord, searching all the inward parts of the belly." —Proverbs 20:27

Children of God can expect to be led by the Spirit of God.

Another translation of Proverbs 20:27 reads, "The spirit of man is the *lamp* of the Lord." Had this verse been written today it might have read, "The spirit of man is the light bulb of the Lord." What it means is: *God will enlighten us, He will guide us, through our spirits.*

Many times, however, we seek guidance by means other than the way God said. When we do, we get into trouble. We sometimes judge how God is leading by what our physical senses tell us. But nowhere does God say that He will guide us through our physical senses. Too often we look at things from a mental standpoint and endeavor to reason out things. But nowhere does the Bible say He will guide us through our mentality. The Bible does not say that the body of man is the candle of the Lord, nor that the mind of man is the candle of the Lord. It says that the spirit of man is the candle of the Lord.

No-No!

9

God will guide us, He will enlighten us, through our spirits.

Now before we can understand how God does lead us and guide us through our spirits we have to understand the nature of man. We have to understand that man is a spirit, that he has a soul, and that he lives in a body.

2

Man: An Eternal Spirit

"And God said, Let us make man in our image, after our likeness: . . . So God created man in his own image, in the image of God created he him;"
—Genesis 1:26,27

Man is a spirit being. He is made in the likeness of God. Jesus said that God is a Spirit (John 4:24). So man must of a necessity be a spirit.

Man is a spirit, he has a soul, and he lives in a physical body (1 Thess. 5:23).

When the physical body of man is dead and in the grave, the spirit lives on. That part of man is eternal. Spirits can never die, and man is a spirit. Paul is speaking of physical death here:

> For I am in a strait betwixt two, having a desire to depart, and to be with Christ; which is far better: Nevertheless to abide in the flesh is more needful for you.
> —Philippians 1:23,24

Paul is going to live. Whether in the body or out of the body, he is still going to live. If he abides, or lives, in the flesh he can teach the church at Philippi and be a blessing to them. That would be more needful for them. It would be far better for Paul himself, however, to depart and be with Christ. Paul was actually saying, "I am going to live in the body or I am going to depart and be with Christ."

11

Who is going to depart?

"*I*" am going to depart. Paul was not talking about his body. His body was not going to depart. Paul is talking about the inward man, the spirit man, who lives inside the body.

People sometimes ask, "Will we know one another in Heaven?"

I always quickly ask, "Do you know one another down here?"

You see, *you* are going to be there. If *you* know one another down here, *you* will know one another there. It is *you* who are here—it is *you* who will be there.

"*I* am going to depart," Paul says, "and be with Christ which is *far better.*" I like that! If he had just said it was better, that would have been good. But he said, "It is *far better!*"

Some false cults teach that when a man dies he is dead like a dog. No, he is not. Man is more than body. He is a spirit, he has a soul, he lives in a body. Others say that when man dies he is in soul sleep. The Bible does not teach that. Some say the spirit does go all right—but it comes back as a cow, or a dog, or someone else. Reincarnation is unscriptural and unbiblical. Stay with the Word of God and it will solve all your problems along this line. Paul said, "*I* am going to depart. *I* am going to be with the Lord, which is *far better.*"

Paul preached the same truths and taught the same facts to all the churches. Here he uses different words to teach the same blessed truth to the church at Corinth:

> . . . but though our outward man perish, yet the inward man is renewed day by day.
>
> —2 Corinthians 4:16

There is an *inward* man. And there is an *outward* man. The outward man is not the real you. The outward man is only the house in which you live. The inward man is the real you. The inward man never grows older. He is renewed day by day. He is a spirit man.

What is our spirit? Keep in mind our beginning texts. Romans 8:14 says, *". . . as many as are led by the Spirit of God, they are the sons of God."* Then the 16th verse gives us a little insight into how the Spirit of God leads us, *"The Spirit (Himself) beareth witness with our spirit, that we are the children of God."* In other words, the Spirit of God bears witness with the spirit of man. Proverbs 20:27 says, *"The spirit of man is the candle of the Lord. . . "* Since according to these Scriptures God will guide us through our spirits, we must find out what our spirit is.

Jesus said to Nicodemus, *"Except a man be born again, he cannot see the kingdom of God"* (John 3:3).

Nicodemus, being natural could only think naturally. So he said, *"How can a man be born when he is old? can he enter the second time into his mother's womb, and be born?"* (v. 4).

Jesus was not talking about a physical birth. He said, *" . . . That which is born of the flesh is flesh; and that which is born of the Spirit is spirit"* (v. 6). He was talking about a spiritual birth.

The part of man that is born again is his spirit. His spirit receives *Eternal Life*—the Life of God, the Nature of God. It is man's spirit that is made a new creature in Christ.

Paul calls him "the inward man." Peter calls him "the hidden man of the heart."

> But let it be the hidden man of the heart, in that which is not corruptible, even the ornament of a meek and quiet spirit, which is in the sight of God of great price.
>
> —1 Peter 3:4

When the Bible speaks of the heart, it is speaking of the spirit. This is the real man. It will help you in your believing and in your faith to think like that. In the New Testament, wherever the word *heart* is used, substitute the word *spirit* and you will get a clearer picture of what it is talking about. It is the spirit of man that is born again.

> Therefore if any man be in Christ, he is a new creature: old things are passed away; behold, all things are become new.
> — 2 Corinthians 5:17

This is talking about the inward man. It couldn't be talking about the outward man. When you are born again and become a new creature you do not get a new body. The outward man is just like it was. If you were bald before you were born again, you are still bald afterwards. If you had brown eyes before, you still have brown eyes. The outward man does not change. God does not do anything with the outward man. (You have to do something with the outward man. You find out what God wants you to do with the outward man from the Bible—and you do it.) God does something with the inward man. He makes the man on the inside a new man in Christ, a new creature, a new creation.

3

Spirit-Conscious

"And the very God of peace sanctify you wholly; and I pray God your whole spirit and soul and body be preserved blameless unto the coming of our Lord Jesus Christ." — 1 Thessalonians 5:23

Paul begins with the inside, the innermost part of man, the heart of his being, which is his spirit, and comes to the outside.

Yet most people misquote this verse. They say, body, soul, and spirit. Why do they put the body first? Because they are more body-conscious than spirit-conscious. Natural things mean more to them than spiritual things. So they put physical things first.

Sometimes we are more mental-conscious because we live more in the mental realm.

But man is a spirit being. We need to be spirit-conscious. Spiritual things will become more real to us the more spirit-conscious we become.

If we are going to be led by the Spirit of God—since we know that God's Spirit leads us through our spirits—we must become more spirit-conscious, or miss out on the whole thing.

Put spirit first. Become more spirit-conscious. Become more conscious of the inward man. Realize you are a spirit being. Realize that in the new birth you became a new creation created by God in Christ Jesus. It will help you grow—*spiritually*.

Many years ago I began to think like this—and at first I would say it to myself out loud: *I am a spirit being. I have a soul. And I live in a body.*

Saying that helped me become more spirit-conscious. It helped my faith. Because faith is of the spirit, or the heart.

4

What is the Difference Between Spirit and Soul?

"For the word of God is quick, and powerful, and sharper than any two-edged sword, piercing even to the dividing asunder of soul and spirit . . . . "
—Hebrews 4:12

The spirit and the soul are not the same.

Many years ago, back in the early 50's, I began an intensive study on this subject. I got books from the leading Bible schools and seminaries, both Pentecostal and denominational, to see what they taught on the subject of man. None satisfied me. None were actually scriptural. They were like the Bible says, "in part." I asked leading Bible scholars and ministers across the nation. You would recognize some of their names if I mentioned them. I even heard someone ask one of the most well-known ministers of today, "What is the difference between the spirit and the soul?" He looked startled and said, "I thought they were the same." That was the answer I got from most of the ministers I asked.

Yet how could they be the same? Paul, by the Spirit of God, said they can be divided by the Word of God. If you can divide them, they cannot be the same.

Only the Word of God can divide the spirit and the soul, however. The reason we have not been able to distinguish

17

between them is we have not dug deep enough into the Word. Years ago, in the western part of the United States, they had what we call "the gold rush." People rushed out west. They were going to get rich in a hurry. Most panned a little gold out of creeks. Some found a few nuggets lying on the ground. But if you really wanted to strike it rich, you had to dig for it. You can skim along on the surface of the Bible and pan out a little gold here and there—and even find a nugget occasionally. But if you really want to strike it rich, you have to dig down into the Word of God.

For 15 years I studied carefully burning the midnight oil. If there was anything I desired to know it was the difference between the spirit and the soul. Eventually, I went through this process of elimination. I wrote it down like this: *With my body I contact the physical realm.* (That goes without argument.) *With my spirit I contact the spiritual realm.* That left only one other part of me that made contact with any other realm. I knew then that it had to be with my soul that I contacted the intellectual realm. So I wrote: *With my soul I contact the intellectual realm.* Here is a Scripture that helped me:

> For if I pray in an unknown tongue, my spirit prayeth, but my understanding is unfruitful.
>
> —1 Corinthians 14:14

The *Amplified* translation reads, "For if I pray in an unknown tongue, my spirit by the Holy Spirit within me prays, but my mind is unproductive . . . ."

Our understanding, our natural human mentality, is a part of our soul.

Notice what Paul said. "My spirit prays, but my understanding is unfruitful." He did not say, "When I pray in an unknown tongue my soul prays." He did not say, "When I pray in tongues, I pray out of my intellect, or out of my mind." He said in effect, "I am not praying out of my soul when I pray in tongues; I am praying out of my spirit, my heart, my innermost being." Do you remember what Jesus said?

> In the last day, that great day of the feast, Jesus stood and cried, saying, If any man thirst, let him come unto me, and drink. He that believeth on me, as the scripture hath said, OUT OF HIS BELLY shall flow rivers of living water.
> (BUT THIS SPAKE HE OF THE SPIRIT, which they that believe on him should receive: for the Holy Ghost was not yet given; because that Jesus was not yet glorified.)
> —John 7:37-39

As a result of receiving the Holy Spirit, Jesus said, out of the belly shall flow rivers of living water. Another translation reads, "out of the innermost being".

A Full Gospel pastor's daughter was 6 years old when she and some of the children were off to themselves one night at a revival. Some of these youngsters were filled with the Holy Spirit and began to speak with other tongues. This little 6-year-old ran up to her mother, holding her stomach, and saying, "Momma, Momma, that came right out of my belly."

She was scriptural. She was speaking in tongues from her belly—her spirit, her innermost being. That's where tongues come from—the Holy Spirit who resides in your spirit gives your spirit the utterance and you speak it out.

Consider these Scriptures together now. *"The spirit of man is the candle of the Lord, searching all the INWARD PARTS OF THE BELLY. . . OUT OF HIS BELLY shall flow rivers of living water. . . ."*

All the leadings I have ever gotten have come out of my spirit—and most have come while praying in other tongues. You can understand why. Your spirit is active when you pray in tongues.

One reason the church world as a whole has failed so

miserably is that it has done so much of just one kind of praying—praying with the understanding, mental prayer. It has endeavored to fight spiritual battles with mental abilities.

I have learned this through these many, many years. In every crisis of life I have learned to look to my spirit inside me. I have learned to pray in other tongues. While I am praying in other tongues, there comes up guidance from inside me. This is because my spirit is active—my body is not active, my mind (my soul) is not active—and it is through my spirit that God is going to guide me.

Sometimes I interpret my praying in tongues, and through the interpretation I receive light and guidance (1 Cor. 14:13). But most of the time, not so. Most of the time, just while I am praying in tongues, from somewhere way down inside, I can sense something rise up in me. It begins to take shape and form. I cannot tell anybody mentally how I know it, because my understanding has nothing to do with it. But I know on the inside of me what to do.

I follow that. I listen to my spirit. Because the spirit of man is the candle of the Lord.

5

The Saving of the Soul

*". . . receive with meekness the engrafted word, which
is able to save your souls."*   —James 1:21

The spirit of man is the part of man that is born again. It is the
part of man that receives *Eternal Life,* which is the Nature and
Life of God. It is the spirit of man that becomes a new creature in
Christ Jesus. The soul is not the innermost being at all. It is not
the soul that is born again. The saving of the soul is a process.

James 1:21 used to bother me when I was a denominational
preacher before I was filled with the Holy Spirit. I didn't know
what I know now. I used spirit and soul interchangeably,
referring to the spirit as the soul, and the soul as the spirit. I
didn't divide them as the Bible does. But I did have enough sense
to leave this verse alone until I grew to where I could
understand what it is saying.

The Epistle of James was not written to sinners. James did
not write a letter to the world; he wrote this letter to the Church.
We know that from James 5 where he says, *"Is any sick among
you? let him call for the elders of the church . . . "* In other words,
is there any sick among the Church, let him call for the elders of
the Church. Also referring back now to the first chapter of
James, let's pick up with verse 18:

> Of his own will begat he us with the word of truth, that we should
> be a kind of firstfruits of his creatures. Wherefore, my beloved

21

brethren, let every man be swift to hear, slow to speak, slow to wrath: For the wrath of man worketh not the righteousness of God. Wherefore lay apart all filthiness and superfluity of naughtiness, and receive with meekness the engrafted word, which is able to save your souls.

—James 1:18-21

James is talking to born-again ones. Of the Father's own will, he writes, we were begotten or born with the Word of Truth. He calls them, "my beloved brethren." So they were in Christ. Yet he encourages these born-again, Spirit-filled people to receive the engrafted Word with meekness, "which is able to save your souls." Evidently, their souls were not saved.

You see, a man's spirit, the innermost man, the real man, receives Eternal Life and is born again. But his intellect and emotions—which compose his soul—still have to be dealt with. They are not born-again. They are to be renewed.

Paul speaks about the renewing of the mind writing to the saints at Rome:

And be not conformed to this world: but be ye transformed by the renewing of your mind, that ye may prove what is that good, and acceptable, and perfect, will of God.

—Romans 12:2

The Psalmist spoke of the restoring of the soul:

He restoreth my soul . . . .

—Psalm 23:3

The Hebrew word translated *restore* in the Old Testament, and the Greek word translated *renew* in the New Testament mean about the same thing. The soul, the mind, is to be renewed or restored.

My mother left me a chair which she inherited from her mother. I don't know exactly how old that chair is, but it is quite old. I can remember, way back there, that my grandmother had it restored. They put new upholstery on it. They revarnished it. It was still the same chair; it was just restored. It was renewed.

It is never written that God restores our spirits. Our spirits become brand new creatures in Christ Jesus. Our souls, however, can be renewed or restored.

How? We have these expressions relative to the soul: *receive with meekness the engrafted word, which is able to save your souls . . . be not conformed to this world: but be ye transformed by the renewing of your mind, that ye may prove what is that good, and acceptable, and perfect, will of God . . . He restoreth my soul.*

Man's soul is saved, or restored, when his mind becomes renewed with the Word of God. It is the Word of God that saves our souls, that renews our minds, that restores our souls.

When our minds get renewed with the Word of God, then we think in line with what God's Word says. We are able to know and prove the permissive and the perfect will of God—because the Word of God is the will of God. We don't have so many questions about the will of God when we get our souls saved.

The greatest need of the Church today is minds renewed with the Word of God.

6

Presenting the Body

"I beseech you therefore, brethren, by the mercies of God, that ye present your bodies a living sacrifice, holy, acceptable unto God, which is your reasonable service." —Romans 12:1

It is the inward man—not the outward man—that becomes a new creature in Christ. We still have the same body we had before we became a new creature. What we must learn to do is to let that new man on the inside of us dominate. With that new man, we control the flesh and do something with our bodies.

Let's look again at Second Corinthians 5:17, *"Therefore if any man be in Christ, he is a new creature: old things are passed away; behold, all things are become new."* One translation reads, *"If any man be in Christ, there is a new self . . . "*

Sometimes in churches we hear people talk about "dying out to self." There is no such statement in the Bible. We don't need to die out to self if we have become a new self. What we need to do is crucify the flesh. The Bible does talk about that.

Crucifying the flesh is not something God does for you. It is something you do for yourself. *"I beseech you therefore, brethren,"* Paul wrote the Church, *"by the mercies of God, that ye present your bodies . . . ."*

Who presents your bodies?

You do.

Who is you?

That's the man on the inside who is born again, and has become a new creature.

You do something with your body. If you do not do something with it, nothing will ever be done.

> But I keep under my body, and bring it into subjection: lest that by any means, when I have preached to others, I myself should be a castaway (disapproved).
>
> —1 Corinthians 9:27

Here Paul is talking about the fact that *he* does something with his body. "*I* keep under my body. *I* bring it into subjection."

Who is *I*?

That's the real man, the real Paul, the man on the inside who has become a new creature in Christ Jesus and is filled with the Holy Spirit. "*I* do something with my body. *I* keep it under. *I* bring it into subjection."

What did he bring his body into subjection to?

To the inward man. Instead of letting the body dominate the inward man, Paul saw to it that the inward man dominated the outward man.

Now notice this. Here is this great apostle, this holy man of God, this man who wrote half the New Testament, a man who is a spiritual giant—yet evidently his body wanted to do things that were wrong. If it hadn't, he would not have had to keep it under. He would not have had to bring it into subjection.

Just because your body wants to do wrong, doesn't mean you are not saved—or, that you are not filled with the Holy Spirit. (If that were the case, Paul was not saved.) You will have to contend with the body, the flesh, as long as you are here.

"Brother Hagin, I want you to pray for me," the man said.

"What for?" I asked. I like to know what I am to pray for.

A look of seriousness, even tears, came to his eyes, "I want you to pray that I will never have any more trouble with the devil."

I said, "Do you want me to pray you will die?"

"No, no, I don't want to die."

I said, "The only way you won't have any more trouble with the devil is to get out of here and go on to Heaven."

You will have problems with the devil as long as you are in this life. You will have problems with the flesh as long as you are in the flesh. But, blessed be God, you have the means, the ability, and the authority given to you through the Word of God to deal with the devil and to deal with the flesh.

Paul did not let his body dominate him. The man on the inside—that was born-again, and filled with the Holy Spirit—dominated the outward man.

You can do it. What I want you to see is this—*you* are the one who must do it. Paul did not say God would do it for you. He did not say the Holy Spirit would do it for you. He said, "*You* present your bodies." He said, "*You* be not conformed to this world." He said, "*You* be transformed by the renewing of your mind."*You* present your body. *You* do it. *You* get your mind renewed with the Word of God. *You* do it.

The Life and Nature of God is inside your spirit. Let that man on the inside be the dominate one. Listen to him. It is the spirit of man that is the candle of the Lord. It is through your spirit that God will guide you.

7

Number One:
The Inward Witness

"The Spirit (Himself) beareth witness with our spirit . . . ."   —Romans 8:16

Y ou will find that being led by an inward witness is the number one, or the primary way, that God leads all of His children.

Let me go back—I said I would in the preface of this book—to what Jesus said to me in February of 1959 in El Paso, Texas. It was 6:30 in the afternoon. I was sitting up in bed studying. My eyes were wide open. (There are three types of visions. The highest type is an open vision. In an open vision one's physical senses are not suspended. His physical eyes are not closed. He possesses all his physical capabilities, yet sees into the realm of the spirit.)

I heard footsteps. The door to my room was ajar 12 to 14 inches. So I looked to see who was coming into my room. I expected some literal physical person. But as I looked to see who it was, I saw Jesus. It seemed as if the hair on my neck and head stood straight up on end. Chill bumps popped out all over my body.

I saw Him. He had on a white robe. He wore roman sandals. (Jesus has appeared to me eight times. Every time except this time His feet were bare. This time He had on sandals; that's what I had heard.) He seemed to be about 5 feet 11 inches tall. He looked to weigh about 180 pounds.

He came through the door and pushed it back almost shut. He walked around the foot of my bed. I followed Him with my eyes—almost spellbound. He took hold of a straight chair and pushed it up close to my bed. Then He sat down in it, folded His hands, and began His conversation by saying, "I said to you night before last in the automobile by my Spirit . . . ."

The automobile was full. My wife and I and others were driving along within two blocks from where I was as Jesus sat by my bedside. I heard the Spirit of God speak to me. I thought everyone in the car heard it. I said, "Did you all hear that?" They said, "No, we didn't hear anything."

In the Old Testament the prophets would say, "And the Word of the Lord came unto me saying . . . ." Did you ever wonder how it came? It could not have been literally audible. If it had been audible everyone present would have heard it—he would not have had to tell them what the Spirit said. The Word of the Lord came to the prophet's spirit from the Spirit of God. It is so real that it seems audible at the time, for it was so real to me I thought everyone with me in the car had heard it too.

Jesus said, as He sat at my bedside, "I spoke to you night before last in the automobile and told you certain things. I told you, by my Spirit, that I would talk to you further later. So now I have come to talk to you about this . . . ."

It was concerning the ministry of the prophet. He sat there in that chair and talked to me for an hour and a half. And I talked to Him. I asked questions in reference to what He was saying. He answered them. I will not go into all He said about the prophet's ministry; that is another message. But I will get into the edge of it.

He said to me, "The prophet of the New Testament is very similar to the prophet of the Old Testament in that the prophet of the Old Testament was called a 'seer' because he saw and knew things supernaturally. The prophet of the New Testament will also see and know things supernaturally. But the prophet of the New Testament does not have the same status as the prophet of the Old, in that I did not set prophets in the Church to guide the Church. One under the New Testament need not seek guidance through prophets. He might receive guidance through prophets, but he should not seek it. It is unscriptural to do so. The ministry of the New Testament prophet in this area is only to confirm what people already have in their own spirits.

"Under the Old Covenant, only the priest, the prophet, and the king were anointed by the Holy Spirit to stand in those offices. What you would call the laity did not have the Spirit of God upon them or in them. Therefore, under the Old Covenant, they would seek guidance through the prophet because he had the Spirit."

Under the New Testament, thanks be to God, we not only have the Spirit of God upon us—we have Him in us!

Jesus said to me, "Under the New Covenant, it does not say, 'As many as are led by prophets, they are the sons of God.' The New Testament says, 'As many as are led by the Spirit of God, they are the sons of God.' "

Then He said, "The number one way, the primary way, that I lead all of my children is by the inward witness. I am going to show you how that works so you won't make the mistakes you have made in the past."

He explained to me that to stand in the office of the prophet, one is first of all a minister of the Gospel separated and called to the ministry with the calling of God upon his life. Secondly, he has at least two of the revelation gifts—the word of wisdom, the word of knowledge, the discerning of spirits—plus the gift of prophecy, operating in his ministry.

Then He called my attention to something that had been happening the previous three days. For the past three days I had sat down to write a letter to a pastor confirming a date to hold a meeting for him. Somehow, the first day, I got about half a page written, then I tore it up and threw it into the wastebasket. The next day I did the same thing. The third day I did the same thing. Now the Lord is here.

He said, "You see me sitting here talking to you. This is a manifestation of the Spirit called discerning of spirits. (Discerning of spirits is seeing into the spirit realm.) This is the prophet's ministry in operation. You are seeing into the realm of the spirit. You see me. You hear me talking. I am bringing you through the vision a word of knowledge, and also a word of wisdom. I am telling you not to go to that church. The pastor would not accept the way you would minister when you got there. But I am never going to lead you this way again. (He never has. That has been 20 years ago.) From now on, I'm going to lead you by the inward witness. You had the inward witness all the time. You had a *check* in your spirit. That's the reason you tore up the letter three times. You had a *something* on the inside, a *check*, a *red light*, a *stop signal*. It wasn't even a voice that said, 'Don't go.' It was just an *inward intuition*."

Then He reminded me of another invitation. I had preached a convention for one of the Full Gospel denominations the previous year. Nearly every pastor there asked if I would come and hold a meeting. I had hundreds of calls, I suppose.

One fellow came up to me and said, "Brother Hagin, do you ever go to small churches?"

I said, "I go anywhere the Lord says to go."

"Well, we only run 70 to 90 in Sunday School. But if God ever speaks to you, we want you to come."

I dismissed that along with hundreds of others. Several months later, however, while praying in the church one day about my services that night, that conversation came back to me. Then every day it continued to come back to me. Finally, after about 30 or 40 days, I said, "Lord, do You want me to go to that little church for a meeting?"

The more I would pray about it, the more I would think about it, as we say, the better I would feel on the inside of me. It wasn't a physical feeling, but one in my spirit.

Sitting by my bedside, Jesus referred to this, "The more you thought about it, the better you felt about it. You had a *velvety-like* feeling in your spirit. That's the *green light*. That's the *go-ahead signal*. That's the *witness of the Spirit* to go. Now you see me sitting here, you hear me talking to you, and I am telling you to go to that church. But I am never going to lead you to go anywhere again like this. (He never has.) From now on, I am going to lead you just like I do every other Christian—by the inward witness."

Then the Lord said this to me, which is not just for my benefit, but for yours, "If you will learn to follow that inward witness I will make you rich. I will guide you in all the affairs of life, financial as well as spiritual. (Some think He's only interested in their spiritual atmosphere, and nothing else. But He's interested in everything we are interested in.) I am not opposed to my children being rich. I am opposed to their being covetous."

I have followed that inward witness and He has done just what He said He would. He has made me rich.

Somebody asked, "Are you a millionaire?"

I didn't say that. They failed to realize what the word *rich* means. It means a full supply. It means abundant provision. I have more than a full supply. I have more than an abundant provision. It is because I learned to follow the leading of the Spirit by the inward witness.

What He did for me, He will do for you. It won't come overnight, or by next Saturday night. But as you learn to develop your spirit and follow that inward witness, He will guide you in every area of your life.

I knew a man down in Texas. At the age of 12 he had never had on a pair of shoes. He had only a 5th grade education. But way back when money was money, he was a millionaire.

Two different people, one from California, the other from Minnesota, who had been frequent house guests in his home, told me this man told each of them the same thing.

He said to them both, "In all these years and investments (that's how he made his money), I have never lost a dime."

That beats my record. How about yours?

"I have never invested in anything but what made it," he told each of them on different occasions. Then he told them how he did it.

"I always do this. When someone comes along with an idea wanting me to invest in something, my first reaction is mental. Now I know when Jesus said, 'When you pray, enter into your closet,' that He didn't necessarily mean you have to get into a closet to pray. I know He meant for us to shut things out. But I have a large closet off my bedroom which I go into and pray about it. I wait long enough until I hear what my spirit says. Sometimes I wait three days. Now I don't mean that I stay in there 24 hours a day. I might come out and eat one meal. Usually I miss a few. I come out and sleep a little bit. But the majority of the time I am waiting, just by myself, until I know inside by an inward witness.

"Sometimes my head says, 'Boy, you would be a fool to put your money in that. You'll lose your shirt.' But my heart says, 'Go ahead and invest in it.' So I do. And in all these years, I have never lost a dime.

"Then again, somebody comes along with a deal and my head says, 'Boy, you had better get in there.' But I don't pay any attention to my head. I get into that closet and wait. Sometimes all night long I wait. I'll pray and read my Bible, but a lot of the time I just wait. I just get quiet until I can hear inside what my heart says. When my heart says, 'No, don't do it,' and my head says, 'Yes, you'd better get in on it,' I don't get into it."

What had he done? He had learned to follow the inward

witness and God had guided him in his business until in the late 30's and the early 40's he was already worth two million. That doesn't sound so big now, but it was big then.

Do you think God loved him more than He loves you? No, he took time to listen to God. He took steps and means and measures to wait.

A group of we ministers were talking personally, conversing with one another. Someone asked a certain individual, I won't mention his name, but he is a very successful minister, "Now we know that God called you and that the anointing of God's Spirit is upon you. But from your standpoint, is there any one thing you do that you would say contributed more to your success than any other one thing?"

That man said, "I always follow my deepest premonitions."

What was he saying? He was simply saying, "I always listen to my spirit. I do what my spirit tells me to do. I follow that inward witness."

The inward witness is just as supernatural as guidance through visions and so on; it is just not as spectacular. Many people are looking for the spectacular and missing the supernatural that is right there all the time.

8

Know-So Salvation

"He that believeth on the Son of God hath the witness in himself: . . . ."
—1 John 5:10

*"F*or as many as are led by the Spirit of God, they are the sons of God"* (Rom. 8:14). The sons of God can expect to be led by the Spirit of God. Hallelujah! They are not led by somebody else telling them what to do. The Holy Spirit is going to lead us. We have the Scripture that says so.

How does He lead? The 16th verse gives us a clue. *"The Spirit (Himself)* **beareth witness** *with our spirit, that we are the children of God"* (Rom. 8:16).

If in this most important aspect of life, the most important thing that can happen to you—becoming a child of God—if the way He lets you know that you are a child of God is by His Spirit *bearing witness* with your spirit, then you can understand that the first and foremost way He will lead you is by the inward witness.

You do not know that you are a child of God because somebody prophesied you are. You wouldn't accept that. You do not know that you are a child of God because somebody said, "I feel like you are." You wouldn't accept that. You are not a child of God because you had a vision. You might, or you might not have had a vision. But that does not make you a child of God. That is not what the Bible says. It is not the way you know that you are a child of God.

How does the Bible say we know we are children of God? *His Spirit, God's Spirit, bears witness with our spirits.*

Sometimes you can't really explain how you know. But you just know, right down on the inside of you. You know it! You know it by the inward witness.

I was born again as a teenager on the bed of sickness April 22, 1933. Since that day the thought has never occurred to me that I might not be saved. Yet even as a young Christian I ran into people who said, "You're not saved because you don't belong to our church." Or those who would argue, "You're not saved because you haven't been baptized our way." And everything else in the world.

But none of it disturbed me. I laughed at it. *Because I had the witness! And I had the love!*

> We know that we have passed from death unto life, because we love . . . .
>
> —1 John 3:14

9

Fleeced!

*"A new heart also will I give you, and a new spirit will
I put within you: and I will take away the stony heart
out of your flesh, and I will give you an heart of flesh.
And I will put my spirit within you . . . ."*
— Ezekiel 36:26,27

In 1941 I didn't know as much as I know now. Please don't
misunderstand me; I don't know as much now as I am going to
know. I would hate to think I know all I am ever going to know in
this life about God and about the Bible. No, we don't know
everything, but praise God for what we do know.

My wife and I were pastors of a church in the black land of
North Central Texas. Another church down in the oil field of
East Texas wanted me to come try out as pastor. So I drove down
and preached one Sunday. The church asked if they could vote
on me for pastor, and I said yes. Traveling back home after the
service, I put out a fleece.

Now I was born and raised Southern Baptist. I started
preaching as a Southern Baptist. In 1937 I was baptized in the
Holy Spirit as a Baptist preacher. In 1939 I accepted the
pastorate of a little Full Gospel Church. It was in March of 1941
that this church in East Texas wanted to consider me as pastor. I
had been around Full Gospel people long enough now that some
of their misconceptions had rubbed off on me. Don't misunderstand me; a lot of good things rubbed off on me too. But

this one was bad. I kept hearing them talk about putting out fleeces. So I put out a fleece.

I really knew better. But it would save me a lot of the trouble of praying, and getting alone and waiting on God, and maybe some fasting, just to put out a fleece.

In putting out a fleece one prays something like this, "Lord, if you want me to do this—You do that." Or, "God, if you want me to do this, then have that happen." Or, "Lord, shut that door, and open this door."

Wrong!

Some of those doors the devil might shut, and the devil might open. They are on his territory. The Bible calls him the god of this world (2 Cor. 4:4). That would be like praying, "Lord, if you want me to go to Kansas City next week, You open Brother Hagin's front door." I might open it myself. I live there. Satan can move in the sense realm.

God has a better way of leading His children than a hit-and-miss method. The New Testament does not say, "As many as are led by fleeces, they are the children of God."

"Yes," someone might say, "but Gideon put out a fleece back in the Old Testament."

Why go back under the old covenant? We have something better. The old covenant is for spiritually dead people. I am not spiritually dead. I am alive! I have the Spirit of God in me.

Remember Gideon was not a prophet, a priest, or a king. Only those, under the old covenant, were anointed by the Spirit of God. The Spirit of God was not personally present with the rest of the people.

That's why every male had to present himself at the temple in Jerusalem once a year. The Shechinah Glory, the Presence of God, was kept shut up in the Holy of Holies. But when Jesus died on Calvary, the curtain that curtained off the Holy of Holies rent in twain from top to bottom—and God moved out. He has never dwelled in earth-made houses since. He dwells in us!

It is dangerous for New Testament, Spirit-filled Christians

to put out fleeces. I know that from the Word. And I know it from experience.

Back there in 1941 I said, as I drove along, "Lord, I am going to put out a fleece. I am just going to turn it over to You. (I didn't realize that I didn't turn it over to the Lord.) If they elect me 100 percent, I am going to accept that as being the will of God, and I am going to accept that church."

I got every vote. That was my fleece. They elected me 100 percent. They missed God. I missed God. They got fleeced. I got fleeced. I got out of the perfect will of God—and God just let me do it.

We moved into the parsonage. Many things were more comfortable than what we had before from the natural standpoint. We had more money. We lived in a better parsonage. We drove a better automobile.

But I would study and pray and get a message—and be just all on fire. Then the minute I stepped inside the church door, it was as though somebody poured a bucket of cold water on me. I lost it all. In 14 months I didn't preach a decent sermon. No inspiration.

My wife was reluctant to say anything. She finally did say, "Honey, you've got to where you can make a pretty good talk."

That was all I was doing, making talks. I wasn't preaching. When my agreed upon time was up, I left. I didn't wait for some signal to leave; I left.

Later on in pastoring, I always wanted to go back there for a meeting because I wanted those people to know I could preach. They had never heard me. So I went back and held a revival. Folks' mouths fell open, "We didn't know you could preach like that."

I said, "Oh, yes, I preached like that before I came here to pastor. I preached like that after I left here."

"Well, you didn't preach like that here."

I said, "No, we were all out of the will of God. I was here out of the will of God. You elected me out of the will of God."

I learned about that fleece business. One time ought to cure a fellow. But some folks, even though none of them have ever worked, still put out fleeces.

I never did miss it anymore in going to any church as pastor. And I didn't put out fleeces. I prayed and waited on God. I talked to God long enough until I knew right on the inside what to do.

10

Following the Witness

*"For thou wilt light my candle: the Lord my God will
enlighten my darkness."* —Psalm 18:28

We left that church. We were asked by leaders of a denomination to take another church to fill in temporarily, so we did.

While I would be in my study praying, I would get a burden to go back to the church I'd left as a result of the fleece. I hadn't finished what God wanted me to do there.

Usually this happened when I was praying about my sermon and the Sunday services in other tongues—and remember, when I pray in tongues my spirit prays, and the spirit of man is the candle of the Lord. I would get such a burden for the church I had left more than two years before, I would jump up and run out of the room to get away from it.

Once I came to myself out in the street beside the church wondering, "How did I get out here?" To get out there I'd had to run out of the church study, across the auditorium, and out the side door. But I didn't remember doing that. I was under such a burden for that church, and I was trying to get away from it. I didn't want to go back there to pastor.

Finally, after about 30 days of that, I said, "Lord, are You talking to me about going back there? Are You trying to give some guidance?" Then I said, "Talk to my wife. She can listen, too."

One morning, while we washed dishes, I said to my wife, "Honey, if the Lord says anything to you, let me know." I didn't tell her anything more.

Then I waited 30 days. You don't have to get into a big hurry about some things. The Bible says, " . . . *he that believeth shall not make haste*" (Is. 28:16). Faith doesn't get in a hurry. The devil will try to push you. He will say, "Hurry up. Hurry up. Hurry, hurry, hurry." He will try to move you out of faith, move you into doubt, move you into unbelief, and get you away from the leading of God.

Thirty days later, as I washed the dishes and she dried, I said, "Has the Lord been talking to you?"

"If He has, I don't know it."

I got a little more pointed to bring her out. I said, "Has the Lord said anything to you about going back to . . . . ?" I called the name of the city where the church was.

"Oh," she said, "I thought that was just me."

"Well," I said, "let's analyze what you mean when you say *me*."

If you mean the flesh, then it wouldn't be right. But if it is the real *me*, the real *you*, the man on the inside, remember that the spirit is the candle of the Lord. Then it is not just you, *it is the Lord lighting the candle.*

"I want to ask you a question," I said to her, "so we can ascertain just what it is. From the physical, from the mental, just naturally speaking, do you want to go back there?"

"Oh, no!"

"It couldn't be you then, could it? (It would have been better to say, it couldn't have been the flesh, the natural man, the outward man.) You're not going to be thinking about doing something you don't want to do."

I saw she had the inward witness just as I did. Sometimes the inward witness is there and people don't recognize it.

"I am convinced," I told her, "that God is leading us that way. It will have to be God to open it up and get us back there. Let's just let Him do it."

He did. Within a few months, without my doing anything to work it out, I was invited to preach a week in that church. Afterwards the board asked if I would be interested in coming back to pastor.

I didn't tell them I had something from God. I just said, "I might be."

They said, "We have all been talking and the church wants you back."

"Well," I said, "they would have to vote on me. So I'll tell you what I'll do—just go ahead and vote, and I will tell you afterwards."

From the natural standpoint my wife and I still did not want to go back. Though we loved the people, we did not want to live in that town. We did not want to live in that house. In my heart I wanted to obey God, but everything about my flesh recoiled. My natural man, my outward man, and in my own natural human thinking and mind, I did not want to go.

So really, when I kept praying and fasting while the church board was making all the proper announcements and advertising the election, I was saying to the Lord that I didn't want to trust that inward witness I knew both my wife and I had.

I was over into the third day of a fast. I wanted the Lord to move in some *supernatural* way—I wanted some kind of a word, tongues and interpretation, a prophecy, or God just to write up in the sky, "GO TO THAT PLACE." I was on my knees bawling and squawling and begging—because I didn't know any better.

God also leads by an inward voice as well as by an inward witness. That inward voice said, "Get up from there and quit acting like that."

I got up. Then I said, "Lord, if You could just give me some supernatural sign, I would feel better about this."

He said, "You have all I am going to give you. You don't need any supernatural sign. You don't need any supernatural writing in the sky. You don't need any tongues and interpretation. You don't need any prophecy. You know on the inside of you what to do. Now do it!"

I said, "Okay, I will."

Many times we ignore the inward witness. We want something out in the sense realm. We seek the sensational and miss the supernatural.

Let's learn that God leads all of His children, *primarily,* by an inward witness.

11

Number Two: The Inward Voice

"I say the truth in Christ, I lie not, my conscience also bearing me witness in the Holy Ghost," —Romans 9:1

The number one way the Spirit guides is through the inward witness. Number two is by the inward voice.

The inward man, who is a spirit man, has a voice—just as the outward man has a voice. We call this voice *conscience*. We call this voice the *still small voice*.

Your spirit has a voice. Your spirit will speak to you.

In September 1966 we moved to Tulsa, Oklahoma from Garland, Texas, a suburb of Dallas. We had lived there 17 years. The move came about like this. My wife and I were in Tulsa on business. The ministry was growing and I had already figured out in my head what I would do with my office and home in Texas. But the friend with whom we were staying in Tulsa said, "Brother Hagin, you ought to move to Tulsa. Brother T. L. Osborn's old office building is for sale. His business manager asked me to sell it for them." Then he quoted their price. It was extremely low. But I was not interested. Finally, he said, "Let's go look at it." I went along just to humor him.

The minute I stood inside that building a buzzer went off inside me. (Sometimes that inward witness is like an inward buzzer.) I knew as well as I knew my name, *this is it*! But I didn't want to listen to it; I wanted to stay in Garland.

(That's why we don't hear a lot of times. We don't want to hear. We say we do, but we don't.)

Back at our friend's home my wife asked me about it.

"Oh, no. I've already got it all figured out. We'll stay where we are. We'll turn our whole home into an office. And we'll just stay in Garland."

We went to bed. But I couldn't sleep.

Ordinarily, I have no trouble sleeping. The Bible says, ". . . *he giveth his beloved sleep*" (Ps. 127:2). I am His beloved. So are you. *"He hath made us accepted in the beloved"* (Eph. 1:6). So I always claim the promise of God and say, "Lord, I'm Your beloved. So I'll take it. I thank You for it." And I always go to sleep.

But this time, I couldn't. My conscience was hurting. My conscience is the voice of my spirit. My spirit knows I didn't listen to it.

Lying there quietly in the nighttime, I said, "Lord, if you want me to move to Tulsa, I will. In the natural, I don't want to move up here, but I wouldn't want to stand in Your way."

Then on the inside of me I heard the still small voice.

Now I'm not talking about the Spirit of God speaking. When the Holy Spirit speaks it is more authoritative. The still small voice is the voice of our own spirit speaking. But our own spirit picks it up from the Holy Spirit who is in us.

That still small voice, that inward voice, not authoritative, just something on the inside of me said, "I am going to give you that building."

I laughed. I know there is a lot of unbelief about this, but I said, "Okay. When you do, I'll believe it."

That inward voice said, "You watch me."

Without going into all the detail, it would surprise you how God gave us that building.

12

Conscience: Voice of the Human Spirit

"And Paul, earnestly beholding the council, said, Men and brethren, I have lived in all good conscience before God until this day." — Acts 23:1

It is interesting to go through the Epistles Paul wrote to the Church and see what he said about his conscience. You will notice that he always obeyed it.

Is your conscience a safe guide?

Yes—if your spirit has become a new man in Christ. Because your conscience is the voice of your spirit.

> Therefore if any man be in Christ, he is a new creature: old things are passed away; behold, all things are become new.
> — 2 Corinthians 5:17

These things take place in man's spirit, in the inward man. He is first a new creature—a brand new man in Christ. Secondly, old things have passed away—the nature of the devil in his spirit is gone. Thirdly, A-L-L things have become new—in his spirit, not in his body and mind—now he has the Nature of God in his spirit.

Therefore, if your spirit is a new man with the Life and Nature of God in it, it is a safe guide.

A person who has not been born again could not follow the voice of his spirit. His spirit is unregenerate. His conscience would permit him to do anything.

When you have the Life and Nature of God in you, your conscience will not permit you to do just anything. And if you are born again, you have the Life of God.

> For God so loved the world, that he gave his only begotten Son, that whosoever believeth in him should not perish, but have EVERLASTING LIFE.
>
> —John 3:16

> For the wages of sin is death; but the gift of God is ETERNAL LIFE through Jesus Christ our Lord.
>
> —Romans 6:23

Somebody said, "That means we are going to live forever up in Heaven."

No, it does not. Consider this Scripture:

> These things have I written unto you that believe on the name of the Son of God; that ye may know that YE HAVE ETERNAL LIFE . . . .
>
> —1 John 5:13

Have is present tense. We have *Eternal Life* now. If you are a born-again Christian, you have the *Life of God* in your spirit. You have the *Nature of God* in your spirit.

Oh! If people would learn to follow their spirits! If they would learn to take advantage of the Life that is in them!

I joined the church and was baptized early in life—but that didn't make me a Christian. My spirit was still unregenerate when I became totally bedfast from a heart condition at the age of 15. I was truly born again during the 16 months I was bedfast. Then in August of 1934, as a Baptist boy reading Grandma's Methodist Bible, I was healed.

I went back to high school. I had missed one school year. Before I was born again, I just barely got by in some classes. Then, if you made a "D" it was failing. And if you failed one subject you stayed in that grade and took the whole thing over again. Two teachers in two subjects said to me, "We gave you two points or you would have had a 'D'."

But after I was born again, I never made anything but a straight "A" report card. And I never took one book home to study.

Now I didn't know a thing about the baptism of the Holy Spirit then, but do you know what I did know? I knew I had the Life of God in me!

As I walked down the street to school every morning —unconsciously, I was being led by the Spirit; my heart told me to do it, and I listened to my heart instead of my head—I had a conversation with the Lord.

I said, "Now, Lord, I read in the Old Testament where Daniel and the three Hebrew children were in school in Babylon and You gave them favor with the dean of the school (Dan. 1:9). God, give me favor with every teacher. Thank You for it; I have it now. Then when their three years of training were over, they were ten times smarter than the rest (vv. 18-20). Lord, I have Your Life in me. John 1:4 says, *'In him was life; and the life was the light of men.'* Light stands for development. Impart to me knowledge and skill in all learning and wisdom that I may be ten times better . . . ."

Every day as I walked to school I would confess, "In Him was Life and the Life was the light of men. That Life is in me. The Life of God is in me. That Life is the light, it is the development of me. It is developing my spirit. It is developing my mentality. I have God in me. I have God's wisdom in me. I have God's Life in me. That Life of God in my spirit dominates me. I purpose in my heart to walk in the light of Life."

Now I do not mean that I just skipped by. In study hall

periods at school I studied. I listened intently in class to everything that was said. But by receiving Eternal Life into my spirit, and getting my mind renewed with the Word, my mentality was increased from 30 to 60 percent.

The Life of God will do that for anybody.

The most amazing miracle I have seen of Eternal Life affecting mentality was in a girl I will call Mary. Her mentality was increased at least 90 percent.

She started to school at seven and went seven years without getting out of the first grade. In those seven years she never learned to write her name. Finally, they asked her parents to take her out of school.

As an 18-year-old, in the church I pastored, I saw her behave like a 2-year-old. She would get down and crawl around on the floor like a baby. If she happened not to be sitting with her mother, she would slide under the pews, or lift up her skirt and step over them, to get to where her mother was. Her clothes were always a sight. Her hair was never combed.

Then one night, during an evangelistic revival meeting, Mary came to the altar. There she received Eternal Life—the Nature of God. A drastic change occurred instantly. The very next night she sat in the service and behaved like any 18-year-old young lady. She had fixed her hair and dressed up. Her mentality seemed to have increased overnight.

Years later I was back in the city to help with a funeral. "What ever happened to Mary?" I asked the church secretary. She led me out on the front porch.

"See all those new houses going up out there."

I said, "Yes."

"That's an addition to the city. Mary is building that. She's a widow now. She handles all her own money. She is her own financier. She has three lovely children. They are on the front pew every Sunday. They are the best-dressed, best-mannered children in church. As church secretary I can tell you that

Mary's tithes and offerings are here every Sunday."

The Life of God came into her!

I am convinced we have never learned what we have received. Most of us have thought that the Lord just forgave us, saying, "We're the same old creature we always were. We'll try to hold out faithful till the end. If we get enough people to pray for us, maybe we can make it."

No, thank God, the Life of God is imparted unto our spirits! The Nature of God is in our spirits. The Holy Spirit is living and abiding in our spirits.

13

Two Experiences

"Then Philip went down to the city of Samaria, and preached Christ unto them . . . when they believed Philip preaching the things concerning the kingdom of God, and the name of Jesus Christ, they were baptized, both men and women . . . Now when the apostles which were at Jerusalem heard that Samaria had received the word of God, they sent unto them Peter and John: Who, when they were come down, prayed for them, that they might receive the Holy Ghost: (For as yet he was fallen upon none of them: only they were baptized in the name of the Lord Jesus.) Then laid they their hands on them, and they received the Holy Ghost." —Acts 8:5,12,14-17

Under the New Covenant every child of God has the Spirit of God. If you are born again, the Spirit of God is in your spirit.

We do need to differentiate between being born of the Spirit and being filled with the Spirit. The born-again Christian can be filled with the Spirit that he already has in him. And when he is filled with that Spirit, there will be an overflowing. He will speak with other tongues as the Spirit gives him utterance (Acts 2:4).

Bible scholars know that water is a type of the Spirit of God. Jesus Himself used water as a type of the Spirit. He used it as a type of the new birth when talking to the woman at the well of Samaria:

> Jesus answered and said unto her, If thou knewest the gift of God, and who it is that saith to thee, Give me to drink; thou wouldest have asked of him, and he would have given thee living water. The woman saith unto him, Sir, thou hast nothing to draw with, and the well is deep: from whence then hast thou that living water? . . . Jesus answered and said unto her, Whosoever drinketh of this water shall thirst again: But whosoever drinketh of the water that I shall give him shall never thirst; but the water that I shall give him shall be in him a well of water springing up into everlasting life.
>
> —John 4:10,11,13,14

He also used water as a type of the Spirit in the infilling of the Holy Spirit:

> In the last day, that great day of the feast, Jesus stood and cried, saying, If any man thirst, let him come unto me, and drink. He that believeth on me, as the scripture hath said, out of his belly shall flow rivers of living water. (But this spake he of the Spirit, which they that believe on him should receive: for the Holy Ghost was not yet given; because that Jesus was not yet glorified.)
>
> —John 7:37-39

These are two different experiences. The new birth is a *well of water* in you, springing up into everlasting life. The infilling of the Holy Spirit is *rivers*—not just one river. The water in the well is for one purpose. The water in the rivers is for another. The water in the well is for your own benefit. It blesses you. The rivers flowing out of you bless somebody else.

Some people say, "If you are born of the Spirit, you have the Spirit, and that's all there is." But no, just because you have had one drink of water is no sign you're full of water. There is the experience subsequent to the new birth of being filled with the Spirit—and as a result, out of the belly (the spirit) rivers of living water can flow.

Others say that people who are not filled with the Spirit and speaking with other tongues do not have the Holy Spirit. That is not true. If I drink half a glass of water, I may not be full, but at least I have water in me. If one is born of the Spirit of God, he has the Spirit of God abiding in him.

14

God Inside

*" . . . for ye are the temple of the living God; as God
hath said, I will dwell in them, and walk in them; and
I will be their God, and they shall be my people."*
— 2 Corinthians 6:16

If you are born again, the Holy Spirit is living and abiding in
your spirit.

He's living and abiding where? In your head? No. In your
body? In a sense, yes, but not exactly the way we think. The only
reason your body becomes the temple of the Holy Spirit is
because your body is the temple of your own spirit. He abides in
your spirit. And He communicates with you through your spirit.

He does not communicate directly with your mind—He is
not in your mind. He is in your spirit—He communicates with
you through your spirit. Of course, your spirit does reach and
influence your mentality.

Even as a newborn babe in Christ, still bedfast, I would know
things by an inward witness. I knew nothing about being filled
with the Holy Ghost and speaking with other tongues—but I
was born of the Spirit. I had the witness of the Spirit right on the
inside of me that I was a child of God.

I had been bedfast about four months when my mother came
to my bed one day and said, "Son, I hate to bother you, but
something is wrong with Dub."

Dub is my oldest brother. He was 17 at the time and he was

59

gone. We didn't know exactly where he was.

She sensed something in her spirit. She thought maybe he had gotten into trouble and was in jail. She said, "I've been praying for him for three days, but I need some help."

I said, "Momma, I thought you already had enough problems with me bedfast. I've been knowing that myself for several days. He's not in jail, though. It's not that kind of trouble. His physical life is in danger. But I've already prayed, and he will make it. His life will be spared. I've already got the answer."

I didn't know how to get the answer on healing right then—it was a year later before I was healed. But I knew some things, praise God, and God will meet you as far as your faith goes.

Three days later, Dub came home in the nighttime. You see, it was 1933 and there was no work. Men were out on the streets with no jobs in those great depression days. Dub had gone down to the Rio Grande Valley to look for work. He didn't find any. So he decided to hop a freight train—lots of people were riding the rails in those days—from the back side of the Valley right on through to McKinney.

About 50 miles south of Dallas a railway detective knocked him in the head and threw him off that train going 50 or 60 miles an hour. He went sailing down the track. They burned coal in those days and they would put the cinders along the track. He hit those cinders and went scooting on his back. It's a wonder it hadn't broken his back. It would have if we hadn't known about it by an inward witness and prayed.

He lay out in the ditch, then came to after a while. His shirt was completely torn off, and the seat of his britches was torn out. So he could only move at nighttime. In the daytime he hid out in the trees in the field—it was the time of year he could find fruit—and in the nighttime he walked up the rail toward McKinney. It was night when he got home. Momma put him to bed and he was all right in a few days.

Momma and I were not Spirit-filled Christians—but we

were Christians. And we had a witness in our spirits that something was wrong—an inward intuition. This is something every Christian ought to have. It is something every Christian should develop. We should develop our spirits.

A Full Gospel minister friend of mine in less than ten years time had three serious automobile accidents. People were killed. His wife was almost killed. He was seriously injured. They were healed by the mercy of God. Cars were demolished.

He heard me teach along some of these lines and he said to me, "Brother Hagin, everyone of those could have been avoided if I had listened to that inward intuition."

Yet in similar instances people will say, "I don't know why that happened to such a good Christian. He's a preacher." (Preachers have to learn to listen to their spirits just like you have to learn to listen to your spirit.) Then they lay it off on God and say that God did it.

This preacher said to me, "If I had listened to that inward something—I just had an intuition that something was about to happen—I would have waited a little bit and prayed. Instead I thought, *I'm busy. I don't have time to pray.*"

Many times, if we would have waited, God would have shown us. We could have avoided many things. But let's not moan and groan about past failures. Let's just take advantage of what is ours and see to it that it doesn't happen again. We can do nothing about what is past anyhow. Let's begin to develop our spirits, and learn to listen to them.

The Holy Spirit is abiding in your spirit. It is your spirit that picks up these things from the Holy Spirit and then passes them on to your mind by an inward intuition, or inward witness.

Jesus said, *"If a man love me, he will keep my words: and my Father will love him, and we will come unto him, and make our abode with him"* (John 14:23). In this passage of Scripture, Jesus is talking about the Holy Spirit's coming. Jesus and the Father in the Person of the Holy Spirit come to abide in us. An abode is the place where one lives. Another translation says, "We will come unto him, and make our home with him."

The Holy Spirit, through the Apostle Paul said, *"Know ye not that ye are the temple of God, and that the Spirit of God dwelleth in you?"* (1 Cor. 3:16). Another translation says, "The Spirit of God is at home in you." That's where He lives—in you!

The Bible says, *" . . . for ye are the temple of the living God; as God hath said, I will dwell in them, and walk in them; and I will be their God, and they shall be my people"* (2 Cor. 6:16).

Put those three Scriptures together:

> Jesus answered and said unto him, If a man love me, he will keep my words: and my Father will love him, and we will come unto him, and make our abode with him . . . Know ye not that ye are the temple of God, and that the Spirit of God dwelleth in you? . . . for ye are the temple of the living God; as God hath said, I will dwell in them, and walk in them; and I will be their God, and they shall be my people.
>
> —John 14:23; 1 Corinthians 3:16;
> 2 Corinthians 6:16

We have never yet plumbed the depth of what God is really saying. "I will dwell in them. I will live in them. I will walk in them." If God is dwelling *in* us—and He is—then that is where He will speak to us.

15

Depend On Your Spirit

*"For verily I say unto you, That whosoever shall say
unto this mountain, Be thou removed, and be thou cast
into the sea; and shall not doubt in his heart, but shall
believe that those things which he saith shall come to
pass; he shall have whatsoever he saith. Therefore I
say unto you, What things soever ye desire, when ye
pray, believe that ye receive them, and ye shall have
them."* —Mark 11:23,24

Your spirit knows things that your head does not know.
Because the Holy Spirit is in your spirit.

When medical science gave me up to die as a teenager and
said they could do nothing further for me, I knew somehow that
if there was help for me anywhere it would be in the Bible.

I started with the New Testament because I knew I didn't
have much time. Eventually I came to Mark 11:23 and 24.

When I came to Mark 11:24, something from outside me
somewhere said to my mind, *That doesn't mean what things
soever ye desire physically, or materially, or financially. That
just means whatsoever things you desire spiritually. Healing has
been done away with.*

I tried to get my pastor to come and tell me what Mark 11:24
did mean. He did not come. One preacher finally did come. He
patted my hand, put on a professional voice and said, "Just be
patient my boy, in a few more days it will all be over."

I accepted the verdict and lay there expecting to die. It was two months before I got back into the Bible and back to Mark 11:23 and 24.

I said, "Lord, I tried to get somebody to help me and I couldn't. So I am going to tell you what I am going to do. I am just going to take You at your Word. When You were here on earth, You said it. I am going to believe it. If You didn't lie about it, I am coming off this bed. Because I can believe what You said I can believe."

Then I hit on this idea. (It took me a long time because I had limited use of my hands. They propped the Bible in front of me and I scooted the pages.) I decided to run my reference on *faith* and *healing*. I came to James 5:14 and 15:

> Is any sick among you? let him call for the elders of the church; and
> let them pray over him, anointing him with oil in the name of the
> Lord: And the prayer of faith shall save the sick, and the Lord shall
> raise him up; and if he have committed sins, they shall be forgiven
> him.
>
> —James 5:14,15

I thought all the rest of the healing Scriptures and prayer promises hinged on that—I thought you HAD to call for the elders of the church. (You don't have to—you just can if you need to.) So I began to cry, "Dear Lord, if I have to call for the elders of the church to anoint me with oil to be healed, then I can't be healed. I don't know any elders of the church that believe in that."

I had been saved about six months, and I had never heard an inward voice. I am not talking about the voice of the Spirit of God—that is more authoritative—I am talking about that still small voice of my spirit.

My spirit said to me, "Did you notice that verse said that the prayer of faith shall save the sick?"

I had to look again. I'd had my mind on the elders and had missed that. "Yes," I said aloud, "that is what it says!" It came as a real shock to me.

Then on the inside of me these words were spoken, "You can pray that prayer as well as anybody can." Hallelujah!

But my spiritual education was slow—just like yours. I stayed in that bed nine more months before I finally saw that I had to believe I received my healing before it was manifested.

It was while I was praying and saying, "I believe that I receive my healing," that I saw what I must do. I said, "I believe that I receive healing from the top of my head to the soles of my feet." Then I began to praise God because I believed that I received my healing.

Again, on the inside of me, I heard these words—this was not that authoritative Voice, but just a still small voice, so faint I would not have heard it if my mind and body had been very active—"Now you believe that you are well."

I said, "I sure do."

That inward voice said, "Get up then. Well people ought to be up at 10:30 in the morning."

I had been paralyzed. It was a struggle. I pushed myself. Finally I got up to where I was draped over the bedpost. My knees sagged down not far from the floor. I had no feeling from my waist down. But draped over that bedpost I said it again, "I want to announce in the presence of Almighty God, the Lord Jesus Christ, the Holy Spirit, and the holy angels present in this room, and I want to call the devil to record and all evil spirits that may be present in this room, that according to Mark 11:24, I believe that I receive my healing."

When I said that, physically, I felt something. It felt like somebody above me was pouring a pitcher of honey on me. I felt it strike me on the top of my head. It seemed to pile up like honey would, and then it would begin to ooze down over me. It had a warm glow to it. It spread down over my head, down my neck and shoulders, down my arms and out the ends of my fingers, and down my body and out the ends of my toes.

I was standing straight! I have been straight ever since.

But I want you to see this. I listened to my spirit. Faith is of the spirit. Your faith will not work to its fullest until you learn some of these things. Learn to depend on Him that is in you. Learn to develop your own spirit. Have faith in your faith.

16

Tender-Hearted

"For if our heart condemn us, God is greater than our heart, and knoweth all things. Beloved, if our heart condemn us not, then have we confidence toward God." — 1 John 3:20,21

Does the Holy Spirit condemn you if you do wrong as a Christian?

No! It is your spirit that condemns you.

You need to learn that. It's a hard lesson to learn, however, because we have been taught incorrectly.

The Holy Spirit will not condemn you. Why? Because God won't. Study what the Holy Spirit through Paul wrote in the Epistle to the Romans. He asked: Who is it that condemns? Does God condemn? No, it is God that justifies.

Jesus said that the only sin the Holy Spirit will convict the world of is the sin of rejecting Jesus (John 16:7-9).

It is your own conscience—the voice of your own spirit—that knows when you have done wrong.

I have found that even when I do wrong, though my spirit condemns me, the Holy Spirit is there to comfort me, to help me, to show me the way back. You will never read in the Bible where the Holy Spirit is a condemner. Jesus called Him the *Comforter.* The seven-fold meaning of that word from the Greek is brought out in the *Amplified Bible:*

67

> And I will ask the Father, and He will give you another Comforter
> (Counselor, Helper, Intercessor, Advocate, Strengthener and
> Standby) that He may remain with you forever,
>
> —John 14:16 *Amplified*

He is all of those! He will stand by you when nobody else will. He
will help you. He is a Helper!

It is your own spirit that knows the moment you have done
wrong. I am glad I learned that early. It paid off richly for me in
life.

I was barely saved and healed and back in high school when
this incident occurred. I really don't know why it slipped out; no
one in our family used profanity. But we had a neighbor, bless
his heart, who could, as we say in Texas, "cuss" up a storm. You
could hear him all over our end of town. I suppose I picked it up
from him. Anyway, I simply said to one of the boys, "Hell
no . . . something or other."

The minute I said that I knew on the inside it was wrong.
What was it that condemned me? the Holy Spirit? No. It was my
spirit. My spirit, this new creature, this new man doesn't talk
that way. The Life and Nature of God doesn't talk that way. Now
the flesh, the outward man, may want to go on doing some
things that he did, and talking some ways he talked, but you
have to crucify the flesh. A good way to crucify him is to bring it
right out in the open.

I did that right then. I didn't wait until I was moved. In my
heart I said, "Dear God, forgive me for saying that." The young
man I said it to had walked away. I located him and asked him to
forgive me. He hadn't noticed what I'd said; he was used to
people talking that way. But I had to get it right.

It was the voice of my spirit. It was my conscience. My
conscience was tender, and I didn't violate it. Unless you keep a
tender conscience, spiritual things will be indistinct to you.
Because your conscience is the voice of your spirit—and it is

your conscience, the voice of your spirit, that will relate to your mind what the Spirit of God is saying to you down in your heart.

The Bible speaks about Christians even having their conscience seared:

> Speaking lies in hypocrisy; having their conscience seared with a hot iron;
>
> — 1 Timothy 4:2

The first church I pastored was a community church out in the country. I usually went out Saturday night, spent Saturday and Sunday nights, and came back into town on Monday. I stayed quite often in the home of a dear Methodist man. This fine spiritual man, a great man really, was 89 years old. He and I didn't get up as early as the others on his farm. They would be out doing chores or in the field when this older gentleman and I had breakfast together around 8 o'clock.

I didn't drink coffee, but this old gentleman did. Now you could scarcely believe it unless you saw it, but he had one of those old-fashioned coffee pots—this was the mid-30's—sitting on an old-fashioned wood stove with coffee boiling in it. I have seen him take that boiling coffee, pour it into a big thick mug— and it so hot it still simmered after it was in that mug—turn it up to his mouth, and drink the whole cup.

The first time I saw him do it, I hollered. I felt like I was burning.

How could he do that? I couldn't. The tissues of my lips, the inside of my mouth, my throat and esophagus are so tender, just one teaspoonful would have burned all the way down. He drank a whole mug without taking it away from his mouth.

He couldn't do that to begin with though. Through years of drinking it hot, his lips and mouth, throat and esophagus became seared. Then he could drink it, and it didn't bother him.

Spiritually, the same thing can happen.

Learn to keep a tender conscience. Learn the minute you miss it and your conscience condemns you, to correct it right then. Don't wait until you go to church. Immediately say, "Lord, forgive me. I missed it." If you have to, if someone else saw you, tell them. Say, "I did wrong. Please forgive me. I shouldn't have said that."

You will have to keep your spirit tender if you are going to be led by the Spirit.

17

Feelings: Voice of the Body

> *"The Spirit (Himself) beareth witness with our spirit, ..."* —Romans 8:16

Too often people think that the witness this verse talks about is a physical something. It is not. It is a spiritual something. It is the Spirit of God bearing witness with our spirits. He does not bear witness with our bodies. You cannot go by physical feeling.

We confuse things by the way we talk. We say, "I feel God's presence." No, we don't. We sense, spiritually, His presence. Use the word *feeling* advisedly; it leaves the wrong impression that it is a physical feeling. Don't mix the physical with it.

Feeling is the voice of the body.

Reason is the voice of the soul, or the mind.

Conscience is the voice of the spirit.

To go by feeling is to get into trouble. That is the reason so many Christians are up-and-down (I call them yo-yo Christians) in-and-out. They go by their feelings. They don't walk by faith. They don't walk by their spirits.

When they feel good they say, "Glory to God, I'm saved. Hallelujah, I'm filled with the Spirit. Everything is fine." Then they feel bad, their face is long and they say, "I've lost it all. I don't feel like I did. So I must be backslid."

I hear people, bless their hearts, talking about being in the

valley, then being on the mountain, then getting back into the
valley again. I have never been in the valley. I have been saved
45 years and I have never been anywhere but on the mountain
top. You do not have to get down in the valley.

They talk about "valley experiences." I have never had any
valley experiences. Oh, yes, there have been tests and trials, but
I was on the mountain top shouting my way all the way
through—living above it!

A woman we had pastored in years gone by came to a
meeting where we were and told us about her 39-year-old
daughter. They were about to operate on her when they
discovered she had a tumor. Then they also found through
hospital tests that she was a diabetic. They were trying to get
the diabetic condition under control when she went into a coma.
Three doctors said she would never regain consciousness; she
would die.

This mother said, "Will you lay your hands on this
handkerchief?" I did, and we prayed. Then that mother got on a
bus and rode 300 miles back to the hospital where her daughter
lay unconscious. She reached under the oxygen tent and laid the
handkerchief on her chest. The minute it touched her, she
revived. She was healed, born again, filled with the Holy Spirit
and began to talk in tongues, all in one application.

The nurses got excited and called the doctor. The doctor said,
"This is wonderful that she has regained consciousness. But she
must remain quiet." He gave her a shot to quieten her down—
but it never did take effect. She just kept on talking in tongues
and shouting, "I'm healed. I'm healed. I'm healed."

The next day they began to run tests. Her blood was perfect.
She no longer had sugar. Then they couldn't find the tumor. It
had disappeared. After several days they dismissed her.

She told my wife and me sometime later that the doctor said,
"We won't charge you anything. We didn't do anything. A
Higher Power than us did it."

Now, three years afterwards, when she was 42 years old, her sister brought her to our door at 2 o'clock one morning. She had another tumor.

I thought she had come to be healed. So I said, "You can be healed again. We will just lay hands on you."

She said, with tears, "Brother Hagin, I don't really care whether I get healed or not. Really, if I could just get back to where I was with God I would just as soon die and go on to Heaven."

Then I assumed she had backslidden. She looked so sad, I just knew she must have committed some terrible sin. So I said, "The Lord will forgive you . . . " And I went through what the Bible says about that. Then I said, "We'll all just kneel down here by the couch. (My wife and the woman's sister were there, too.) I will kneel beside you. Now you don't have to confess to me, but tell the Lord about it and He will forgive you."

She looked up at me and said, "Brother Hagin, I've searched my heart, and as far as I know, I haven't done anything wrong."

I got aggravated. I'd gotten to bed late—I was driving a distance and holding meetings every night. And just right in the middle of good sound sleep, early in the morning, came this knocking at the door that woke us. I guess I did speak sharply. I know I did.

I said, "Get up out of the floor. Sit down there on that couch." I was disgusted. "If you haven't done anything wrong, what in the world makes you think you have to get back to God?"

"Well," she said, "I don't feel like I did."

I said, "What has that got to do with it? If I were going by feeling, half the time when I get up to preach I would announce that I must be backslidden."

She looked at me. "Do you mean preachers are that way, too?"

I said, "Yes, we're just as human as anybody. And in fact, if I were going by feelings right now, I would be having you pray for me. I don't feel a thing. I haven't felt a thing since you got here."

She said, "What do you do then? How do you pray through?"

I said, "I don't pray through. I'm already through. A Christian ought to walk through—he ought to be through, in fellowship with God, every day, every minute, every hour."

She said, "What do you do then?"

"Well," I said, "just sit there and watch me. I'm going to close my eyes and pray, but you keep your eyes open."

Then I prayed, "Dear Lord, I'm so glad that I'm a child of God. I'm so glad that I'm saved. I'm so glad I have been born again. I don't feel anything—but that has nothing to do with it. My inward man is a new man. My inward man is a new creature in Christ. I want to thank You that not only am I born again—but I am filled with the Holy Spirit. God the Father, God the Son, and God the Holy Spirit reside in me. I want to thank You for that. Hallelujah!"

I didn't feel anything, but I said it anyhow. Then, when I confessed that, in my spirit—He was in there all the time —something began to bubble up inside me. It was a move and manifestation of the Spirit of God. I still did not feel anything. But in my spirit I could sense that bubbling. It got up in my throat. I began to laugh—there is a laugh in the spirit. I began to talk in tongues.

This lady said, "The expression on your face changed. Your face just lit up."

I said, "That was in there all the time. Paul told Timothy to stir up the gift that was in him. I just stirred up what I had in me all the time."

She said, "Can I do that?"

I said, "Yes, you can."

She did—and stirred up what was in her all the time.

I do not remember even praying about the tumor. The last account I had of her, it had disappeared.

Base your faith on the Word—not on your feelings.

Romans 8:16 does not say that the Spirit beareth witness with our bodies, or with our feelings.

Smith Wigglesworth, the great English apostle of faith, said, "I am not moved by what I feel. I am not moved by what I see. I am moved only by what I believe. I cannot understand God by feelings. I understand God by what the Word says about Him. I understand the Lord Jesus Christ by what the Word says about Him. He is everything the Word says that He is."

You cannot understand yourself by feelings. Understand yourself as a born-again, Spirit-filled Christian by what the Word of God says about you. And when you read what the Word says about you—then, whether you feel like it or not, say, "Yes, that's me. I have that. The Word says I have that. I can do what the Word says I can do. I am what the Word says I am."

You will begin to develop spiritually then.

And it is with your spirit that the Holy Spirit bears witness.

18

Help From Within

"Howbeit when he, the Spirit of truth, is come, he will guide you into all truth: for he shall not speak of himself; but whatsoever he shall hear, that shall he speak: and he will shew you things to come."

—John 16:13

Let's notice some things Jesus said about the Holy Spirit.

" . . . he will guide you into all truth . . . . " He will lead you. He will guide you.

" . . . for he shall not speak of himself; but whatsoever he shall hear, that shall he speak: . . . ." He does speak. Whatever He hears God say, whatever He hears Jesus say, He will speak to your spirit. Where is He to speak? He is in your spirit—and that is where He speaks. He doesn't speak out in the air somewhere. It is on the inside. He passes God's message on to your spirit—either by an inward witness, or by an inward voice.

" . . . he will shew you things to come . . . . " I do not believe this just means that the Holy Spirit will show us about future events as recorded in the Word of God. It also means that the Holy Spirit will show *you* things to come. In my own individual life, for instance, there has never been a death in our close family that I did not know about in advance. I knew two years ahead of time that my father-in-law was going to die. So I began to prepare my wife for his death. She was his only daughter, the baby of the family, and very close to her father. I knew she would

take it hard. So I began to say to her, "Honey, you know Mr. Rooker is getting older. He's nearing 70 and God has only promised us 70 or 80 years." Over the two years I dropped a word here and there, just getting her ready.

I was away in a meeting when the telephone call came. After the service one night, I was sitting in the hotel. The phone rang. Something in me said, "That's for you. This is what you have been talking about for two years now." In 28 days he was in Heaven. You are not unprepared when you know things ahead of time.

> But the Comforter, which is the Holy Ghost, whom the Father will
> send in my name, he shall teach you all things, and bring all things
> to your remembrance, whatsoever I have said unto you.
> —John 14:26

The Holy Spirit shall teach you.
He shall bring all things to your remembrance.

People often ask me how I remember things. At one time I could quote three-fourths of the New Testament.

"How do you memorize?"

I always answer, "I never memorized Scripture in my life. I know nothing about memorization. I suppose you could develop your mind if you would work at it. But I just get to talking and it rises up in me. He brings it to my remembrance. He is in there."

The Holy Spirit will show you things to come and bring things to your remembrance if you will learn to cooperate with Him.

19

Number Three: The Voice of the Holy Spirit

"While Peter thought on the vision, the Spirit said unto him, Behold, three men seek thee." —Acts 10:19

God leads us by what we call the still small voice. But He also leads by the Voice of the Spirit of God speaking to us. This is the third most important way we are led by the Spirit. Number one is by the inward witness. Number two is by the inward still small voice. Number three is by the Voice of the Holy Spirit.

There is a difference between the inward Voice of the Holy Spirit speaking to our spirits, and that still small voice which is the voice of our own spirit speaking to us. When the Holy Spirit within you speaks, it is more authoritative.

Sometimes it is so real—although it is inside you—you look around to see who said it. You think somebody behind you said something. Then you realize it was in you.

Remember in the Old Testament how young Samuel heard a Voice call his name, "Samuel, Samuel"? He thought Eli was calling him. He jumped up and ran in to find out what he wanted. Eli said, "No, I didn't call you." Samuel went back to bed. Then again he heard, "Samuel, Samuel." Again he ran to Eli. "No, I didn't call you." It happened the third time. Finally, it dawned on Eli what was happening. He said, "The next time He calls you, answer Him." Samuel answered that Voice, and the Lord spoke to him.

I have found in 44 years of ministry that when God moved in a more spectacular way—all of His leadings are supernatural; some are not so spectacular—when He spoke to me in what seemed to me an audible voice, for instance, there was rough sailing ahead. If He had not spoken so spectacularly I would not have stayed steady.

Concerning the last church I pastored, for example, I heard the pastorate was open and made arrangements to preach there one Wednesday night. During the period of time before I was to go there to preach I held a three-week revival in Houston. During this revival the pastor, his brother (who was also a preacher), and I met at the church every day to pray about the night services. The church with the open pastorate was their home church. Every day they would ask me, "Have you prayed about that church yet?"

Finally, I did. I just said to the Lord, "I'm going up there next Monday and I'm going to preach Wednesday. I don't know whether You want me to pastor there or not. I don't know if I even want to pastor it. But whatever You say about it is fine with me."

That is all I said. Then I heard a Voice speak so plainly I jumped. I looked behind me. I thought really that one of those preachers heard me say it and was joking me. But I heard this Voice. To me it was audible. It said, "You are the next pastor there. And that will be the last church you ever pastor."

(You could interpret that a thousand different ways! You could let the devil tell you, you were going to die. Or that you were going to be defeated. But it meant that my ministry would change to a field ministry.)

About then those two preachers walked down the aisle. As usual, they asked, "Have you prayed about that church yet?"

I said, "You two fellows are looking at the next pastor."

"Oooh, if you knew that church like we know it, you wouldn't say that. It's split right down the middle. Anything half the church is for, the other half is against. It takes two-thirds of the vote to get elected as pastor, and we'll just be honest with you, you can't get elected."

"I don't know about that. I just know I'm the next pastor."

"Well, you don't know that church like we do."

I said, "No, but I know Jesus. And I know the Spirit of God. I know what He said to me."

After I preached the first time, I saw why God moved in such a spectacular way. Every word I spoke bounced right back to me like a rubber ball off the back wall. It was tough.

I thought I was only going to preach one night, but they had arranged that I would preach several nights. Each night we had to move to a different place to stay. We were at one deacon's house one night, another deacon's house the next.

One deacon told us, "If you stayed with me all the time some of the rest of them would probably get jealous and think I'm for you and they would vote against you."

We kept all our things in the car, and every night we would get out just enough for the next day. And every night when we got off to bed, I would say to my wife, "If God hadn't spoken so spectacularly to me, I would just get up, get the children, get into the car, and leave without saying a word to anyone."

My flesh wanted to leave so badly. My mind wanted to leave. My spirit held me steady because God had spoken in such a spectacular way.

They had the election. I got every vote. Everyone said, "It's the greatest miracle of the century—that anybody could get that kind of vote from this church."

I knew all the time I would get it. The Spirit of God told me.

20

Judging By the Word

"Prove all things; . . . ."   −1 Thessalonians 5:21

Always remember this: the Bible teaches that the Spirit of God and the Word of God agree. Anytime the Spirit of God speaks to you it will always be in line with the Word.

People have heard "voices" and gotten every kind of "revelation" you can imagine. Some people are always claiming to hear a voice.

You can, and you should, judge those things. You can judge whether it is right or wrong simply by judging it by the Word.

Several years ago I was preaching in California. A woman who had invited the pastor, his wife, and me to her home for the noon meal said, "Brother Hagin, I want to tell you what the Lord said to me. I want to give you my revelation."

Before she opened her mouth I sensed by the inward witness in my spirit that something was not right. But she persisted, and I agreed. She had fed us in her lovely home, and now she wanted to give me this "revelation." She began to relate it and talked for about ten minutes before I stopped her. I just couldn't stand anymore.

"Please," I said, "wait a minute. There's a Bible there on the table by the chair. Pick it up and open it to. . . ." I gave her a chapter and verse in the New Testament. "Read that."

She read it. Then I gave her another. She read it. I pointed

83

her to several Scriptures. Everything she read contradicted what she said.

I said, "See, I cannot accept what you are saying. It is not in line with this Book. Therefore it cannot be the Spirit of God."

"But, Brother Hagin, I was praying at the altar."

I said, "I don't care if you were praying on top of the church. It's still not right. It is not in line with the Word."

"Yes, but I know God gave this to me."

I said, "No, He didn't. This is His Word and what you are saying is in direct opposition to what the Word of God says. Can you give me any Scripture to substantiate what you are saying?"

"No. But I know I heard the voice speak to me."

"I just gave you five portions of Scripture, and with a little thought I could have given you twenty, that contradict what you are saying."

"Well, yes," she said, "Bible or no Bible, I know God spoke to me and I am going to stay with it."

As we left the pastor said, "I didn't want to say anything to you before, but this dear woman was a fine saint of God, on fire for the Lord. She was a blessing to the church. Now she has been put out of every Full Gospel church in the city because she persists in pushing this off on everybody."

We are not to seek voices.

We should not follow voices.

We should follow the Word of God.

I preached a meeting in Oregon in the summer of 1954. At the close of one of the first services, I was laying hands on the people who stood in the long prayer line. I asked each one what they came for before I ministered to them. When I came to one woman, her husband who had her by the arm said, "We have come for my wife's healing." He told me she had had a mental breakdown.

I did not know this woman was a former Sunday School

teacher in that church, nor that her husband was a deacon.

But when I laid hands on her, just like it ran off on a television screen in a second of time, I knew all this about the situation. I knew it by the spiritual gift called the word of knowledge (1 Cor. 12:8). I saw her in a large tent meeting in one of Oregon's largest cities. I saw her sitting in the congregation with thousands of people. She heard the evangelist tell how God spoke to him in an audible voice and called him into the ministry.

I do not doubt that. She failed to realize, however, that he did not ask God to speak to him that way. God just did it on His own. We have no right to seek that God speak to us in an audible voice. If God told us He would in His Word, then all of us would have a right to claim it. This evangelist didn't even particularly expect God to speak in that way—but if God wants to, He can, and He saw fit to do so.

At the time she heard him tell that, she was all right mentally. But then she began to seek that God would speak to her in an audible voice—and the devil accommodated her. She began to hear voices. They drove her insane. She was now about to be taken to the asylum for the second time.

I also saw this in the spirit. Her husband had taken her to this same evangelist for deliverance. She did not receive deliverance. Now he blamed that evangelist. He had taken her to another leading evangelist. She had failed to be delivered. Now this deacon is angry with him. I knew she would not be delivered if I laid hands on her, and then he would be angry with me. So I took my hand off of her.

I said to the man, "Take your wife into the pastor's study. Wait there. When I finish this line, I will talk with you."

The pastor and I went into the study together.

"First of all," I said, "I have never been to Oregon before. I have never seen you folks. I don't even know if the pastor knows you."

The pastor said, "He's one of our deacons."

"Well," I said, "the pastor will tell you he has not told me anything."

Then I related what I had seen.

The deacon said, "That's exactly right."

"Now," I said, "I will tell you why I didn't minister to her. You see, she wants to hear these voices."

Then I said, "She is not that much gone mentally that she doesn't know what I am saying."

She spoke up, "I know exactly what you are saying."

I said, "Sister, you are not going to be delivered until you want to be delivered. As long as you like it the way it is—as long as you want to hear these voices—you are going to hear them."

She said, "I want to hear them."

As long as a sinner wants to live in sin, God will let him live in sin. But if he wants to change, God will meet him.

And even though a person is a Christian, does not mean he loses his free moral agency. He does not become a robot, a machine where God pushes a button and he automatically has to do whatever He desires. He is still a free moral agent. As long as he wants things like they are, they will stay that way. But if he wants to cooperate with God, he can be helped.

This woman said, "That's the way I want it."

I said, "I knew that the minute I touched you. That's the reason I didn't minister to you. As long as you want it that way, it's going to be that way."

DO NOT SEEK VOICES!

> There are, it may be, so many kinds of voices in the world, and none of them is without signification.
>
> —1 Corinthians 14:10

We are not to accept anything without examining it in the light of the Word of God.

I am glad that I learned some of these things early in life. I mentioned my healing as a young boy just acting on Mark 11:23 and 24.

I was born with a deformed heart. I never ran and played like other children. I became bedfast four months before my sixteenth birthday. My body became practically totally paralyzed. I wasted away until I weighed only 89 pounds.

One day I asked the fifth doctor on the case, "Is something wrong with my eyesight, or with my blood? When Dr. Mathis took blood from my finger, it didn't look red."

This doctor said, "I will tell you the truth, son. And I will explain it to you in layman's terms. The white blood corpuscles eat up the red corpuscles faster than you can build them up, or we, medically, can do anything about it. If you didn't have the heart condition, if you didn't have the paralysis, this incurable blood disease alone would prove fatal."

I knew nothing about divine healing. I didn't know anybody in all the world believed in divine healing. When I found it in the Bible, I thought I had found something nobody else knew anything about. And I acted on God's Word and was healed.

The members of my family were what we call normal Christians. Literally, they were baby Christians. They were saved, but they were not taught beyond that. They were ignorant of the Word of God concerning healing. (Our church taught God could heal, if He would. Others taught not only that He would not, but that He could not.) So when I began to see certain things in the Bible and began to talk to my family about them, they discouraged me. I had enough sense just to stay with the Bible and keep those things to myself.

Nobody was in the room when I received my healing. I had been getting up and walking around the room for a couple of days before I said to Momma, "Bring me a pair of shoes and socks, some underclothes, and a pair of pants and a shirt. (I had worn nothing but bedclothes for 16 months.) I am going to get up and go to the breakfast table in the morning."

"Oh, son, do you know what you're doing?"

It took me 45 minutes to talk her into the notion of laying out those clothes.

We made our home with our grandparents on our mother's side and I asked her not to tell the rest of the family.

Now you could just mark it down. Grandpa got up early and sat out on the porch swing. When you heard that porch swing creak as he got up and headed toward the back of the house to the dining room, there was no use in looking at your watch; it was 7:30. Grandpa ran on schedule. If you did look at your watch, and it didn't say 7:30, you had better set it. It was 7:30.

My bedroom was in the front of the house. At 7:30 that August morning I heard that porch swing creak. I heard his footsteps as he walked to the back of the house. I was already fully clothed, sitting in a chair in my room. I gave them time to get seated at the table. Then I walked out of my room, across another bedroom, and into the dining room.

They did not expect that. Grandpa, a man of few words, looked up and said, "Is the dead raised? Is Lazarus raised up?"

I said, "Yes, the Lord has raised me up."

Then he asked me to offer the blessing. I prayed. And we ate. It is amazing how quickly you can eat if you don't talk so much. You didn't talk at Grandpa's table—especially the young folks. Within 15 minutes we were finished.

I went back to my room. It was 10 minutes till 8 o'clock. I knew Momma would come in about 8 to make up the bed. Usually I was in it and she would give me my bath. Just two days before, the day I was healed, she had bathed me. I was that helpless. So this Thursday morning, even though my heart was beating right, I felt weak from putting out so much energy.

So I thought, *I'm just going to lie down across the bed and rest till Momma comes to clean the room. Then I'll go out and sit with Grandpa in the swing.* I had in mind to walk up town around 10 o'clock.

I dozed off to sleep and slept ten minutes. At 8 o'clock I suddenly became wide awake. I thought Momma was in the room. Somebody was in the room. I didn't see him, but I heard this voice. To me it was audible.

It spoke in a slow, deep monotone and even quoted Scripture. It said, "AND WHAT IS YOUR LIFE? IT IS EVEN A VAPOR THAT APPEARETH FOR A TIME, AND THEN VANISHETH AWAY."

There was a pause.

Then the voice said, "AND TODAY THOU SHALT SURELY DIE."

Every voice is not God. The first audible voice I ever heard was the devil, but I didn't recognize that then. I thought God was right there in that room.

I sat up in the bed. Thoughts came to my mind faster than machine gun bullets fly. I knew James said, "For what is your life? It is even a vapour, that appeareth for a little time, and then vanisheth away" (James 4:14). I knew that was Scripture. And I knew the Lord told Isaiah to tell Hezekiah, "Set thine house in order: for thou shalt die, and not live" (Is. 38:1).

Also, back before I had known about divine healing, for the first six months of being bedfast, I had prayed in the only realm I knew. The doctors had said I had to die and I accepted it. So I prayed, "Lord, just let me know ahead of time so I will have time to tell everybody good-bye."

So these thoughts, like another voice speaking to my mind, said, *God has moved in this supernatural way to let you know you are going to die so you will have time to tell everybody good-bye. Divine healing is right. You have been healed.* (The devil couldn't argue that. I already had the Word on that.) *Your family knows you have been healed. They can see that. But remember, the Bible said, "It is appointed unto man once to die." Your appointed time has come. You are going to die today.*

I got up off the bed—I thought God was standing right in that room—and I tiptoed across the room and sat down in a chair by the window. There I waited, from about 8:30 in the morning until 2:30 in the afternoon, to die.

About 2:30, still sitting in that chair, some words came floating up from somewhere down inside me. I didn't know then what I know now. But I was born of the Spirit. The Holy Spirit was in my spirit. And He is the one who wrote the Bible. Holy men of old wrote as they were moved by the Spirit. The Spirit knows what is in that Book. Because He was in me, then my spirit knew some things that the Holy Spirit knows.

So these words came floating up from somewhere inside me to my mind, *With long life will I satisfy him, and show him my salvation.*

I didn't listen to them. I just let them float away from me. I still sat there waiting to die.

The second time, these words came floating up from inside me to my mind, *With long life will I satisfy him, and show him my salvation.*

I picked them up and turned them over a couple of times in my mind. Then I thought, *Yes, but God has moved in this supernatural way to let me know I am going to die today.* When I got my mind on that, those words disappeared.

The third time, as I sat there, these words came floating up, that inward something said to my mind, *With long life will I satisfy him, and show him my salvation.*

For a moment, I picked them up and repeated them just in my mind. Then I said, in a whisper, "Yes, but God has moved in this supernatural way to let me know that I am going to die." Again, when I got my mind on that, I missed it.

The fourth time, a little more authoritatively, the Spirit of God spoke. I jumped. I thought someone had slipped up behind me. The Voice of the Spirit of God said, "With long life will I satisfy him, and show him my salvation."

I said, "Who said that?" I meant, who is in here talking to me.

But the Voice answered and said, "The 91st Psalm."

My Bible was on the floor under the chair I had been sitting in all day. I hadn't even looked at it. I picked it up now and turned to the 91st Psalm. When I got down to the end, sure enough, it said, *"With long life will I satisfy him, and shew him my salvation"* (v. 16).

But do you think the devil will give up that quickly? Oh, no. Another voice—it seemed like something sitting on my shoulder—said into my natural ear and mind, "Yes, but that's in the Old Testament. That's just for the Jews. That's not for the Church."

I sat there and thought for a moment. Then I said, "I know what I'll do. I will run my references. If I can find anything in the New Testament like that I will know it belongs to me and to the Church."

I started with Psalm 91. A reference to "with long life" led me into Proverbs. Then the Word began to enlighten me. In Proverbs I began to see that the audible voice could not have been God.

The voice had quoted Hebrews 9:27, *"And as it is appointed unto men once to die, but after this the judgment,"* but then had misinterpreted it. Because he knew I didn't know better the voice said, "Everybody has an appointed time to die." You hear people say that all the time. Even born-again, Spirit-filled Christians say, "When your time comes you're going to die." That is not true. You do not have an appointed time to die.

I read in the Book of Proverbs again and again that if you do certain things, your days will be shortened. But doing other things will add unto you length of days. I knew God's Word was right. I knew that even though that voice picked a verse out of a chapter and gave it to me, it was not God. Because it was not in line with the rest of the Word of God.

I continued to run references. This brought me over into the New Testament. I came over to Ephesians 6:1-3. And then into

First and Second Peter. And I found that Paul and Peter quoted the Old Testament concerning long life.

I jumped up out of that chair with my Bible in one hand. I doubled up my fist, kicked with my foot, and said, "Devil, you get out of here. That was you talking to me. That was you that spoke to me in that supernatural voice. I want you to know that I'm not going to die today! And I'm not going to die tomorrow! And I'm not going to die next week! And I'm not going to die next month! And I'm not going to die next year! And I'm not going to die the next 5 years! And I'm not going to die the next 10 years! And I'm not going to die the next 15 years! And I'm not going to die the next 20 years! And I'm not going to die the next 25 years! And I'm not going to die the next 30 years! And I'm not going to die the next 40 years! And I'm not going to die the next 50 years! And I'm not going to die the next 55 years!"

I was 17; that put me up to 72.

He said, "With long life will I *satisfy* thee." If I am not satisfied with life at 72, then I will go on until I am satisfied!

21

My Spirit?
or
The Holy Spirit?

"The spirit of man is the candle of the Lord . . . ."

—Proverbs 20:27

Someone might ask, "How can I tell whether it is my own spirit, or the Holy Spirit telling me to do something?"

The spirit of man is the candle of the Lord.

"But it may just be *me* wanting to do it."

Define your terms. If by "me" you mean the flesh, of course you cannot always obey the flesh. But if by "me" you mean the inward man, the real you, that is all right. Go ahead and do what he wants you to do.

If your spirit is a new creature in Christ Jesus, and old things are passed away, and all things are become new, and your spirit has the Life and Nature of God in it, and the Holy Spirit in it, and your spirit is in fellowship with God, it is not going to tell you to do something that is not right. If you are a Spirit-filled Christian, your inward man has the Holy Spirit in His fullness—not in a measure, in His fullness—making His home in you.

It is not the inward man of the Christian that wants to do wrong—it is the outward man. You ought to be able to tell whether it is the flesh wanting to do something, or the spirit. Here is a text that has been a puzzle to many:

> Whosoever is born of God doth not commit sin; for his seed remaineth in him: and he cannot sin, because he is born of God.
>
> —1 John 3:9

This is talking about the inward man. Physically we are born of human parents and we partake of their nature. Spiritually we are born of God and partake of His nature. God's nature is not the nature to do wrong.

I have missed it a lot of times as a Christian. But my inward man didn't do it. He didn't even agree with me when I did it. He tried to get me not to do it. My heart wept because I did it. My flesh threw me and I missed it, but my spirit never did consent to it. That seed is in my spirit, not in my flesh.

If you continue to allow your flesh to dominate you, you will continue to miss it. If you continue to let your natural mind dominate you, and do not get your mind renewed with the Word, you will continue to miss it.

That's why Paul wrote born-again, Spirit-filled Christians at Rome and told them to do two things: 1. present your bodies, 2. renew your minds with the Word (Rom. 12:1,2).

Until your mind is renewed with the Word of God, your flesh and your unrenewed mind will dominate your spirit. That will keep you a baby Christian—a carnal Christian.

Paul said to the church at Corinth, *"I, brethren, could not speak unto you as unto spiritual, but as unto carnal, even as unto babes in Christ"* (1 Cor. 3:1).

"For ye are yet carnal," he said (v. 3). One translation says, "For you are yet body-ruled."

Then he told them, *"and* (ye) *walk as men"* (v. 3). Another translation says, "Ye walk as mere men." What did he mean? He meant they were walking and doing things just like unsaved men do.

When you get your mind renewed with the Word, then your mind will side in with your spirit instead of your body. And the two of them—your spirit through your mind—will control your body.

My spirit will not tell me something wrong. It has the Nature of God in it, it has the Life of God in it, it has the Love of God in it, it has the Spirit of God in it.

> Whereby are given unto us exceeding great and precious promises: that by these ye might be partakers of the divine nature . . . .
>
> —2 Peter 1:4

We are born of God. Then we feed on the Word of God. By so doing we are partakers of the divine nature, God's nature. If we have the divine nature in us, our spirit will not tell us to do something wrong.

Whatever your spirit tells you will be right.

22

I Perceive

"Now when much time was spent, and when sailing was now dangerous, because the fast was now already past, Paul admonished them, And said unto them, Sirs, I perceive that this voyage will be with hurt and much damage, not only of the lading and ship, but also of our lives." — Acts 27:9,10

Paul said, *"I perceive . . . . "* He did not say, I have a revelation. He did not say, the Lord told me. He said, "I perceive."

How did he perceive it?

By the inward witness. He did not perceive it mentally. He did not perceive it physically. In his spirit he had this witness.

A family of seven went out to eat. The coffee and soft drinks and the children's food had already arrived at the table when the father suddenly said, "Let's rush home."

"Why?"

"I don't know. I just have an urge, a perception, that we should."

They rushed home. A fire had started. If they had waited everything would have burned. But the witness of the Spirit warned them in time.

If it had burned down, someone might have said, "God did that. He had some purpose in it."

No, we have missed it because we didn't listen. We have not been spirit-conscious.

You cannot find anywhere in the Bible where God causes these things to happen to teach them something. If they had listened to Paul they could have saved the ship and the merchandise. As it was, they lost all that and almost lost their lives. They would have lost their lives if they had not started to listen to Paul.

God is not an enemy! He is trying to help us! He is not working against us! He is working for us!

As we become more spirit-conscious we can learn how to better cooperate with Him.

Remember that the primary way God leads His children is by the inward witness.

23

Spectacular Guidance

"Whereupon, O king Agrippa, I was not disobedient unto the heavenly vision:"

—Acts 26:19

God leads us today just like He led the first Christians. His Word works now just like it did then. It has not changed. The Spirit of God has not changed. God does not change.

The early believers did not have one church back then and we have another church now. We have made a mistake in thinking that. We are in the same age they were in—the Church Age. We are in the same Church. We have the same Holy Spirit. It has seemed to us, however, that they had a whole lot we don't have. Not so.

"For as many as are led by the Spirit of God, they are the sons of God." There are sons of God today. And the Spirit of God is still leading sons of God.

So we look into the Acts of the Apostles and elsewhere in the Bible to see how He led them. At times some received guidance through a vision. Others received guidance from an angel who appeared and told them what to do.

Such phenomena, however, did not happen every day in these people's lives. They occurred once or twice in a lifetime for most. So these are not the ordinary ways God leads. We get the impression that nearly every day an angel appeared to somebody and told them something. Not so.

Too many times while God is trying to bear witness with our spirit, trying to guide us the way He said He would in His Word, we do not listen because we want something such as a vision or an angel.

We have no right to seek a vision. We have no right to ask for an angel. There are no Scriptures which say that we should. We do have a right to claim what the Bible promises. If God wants to send an angel, fine. If He wants to give a vision, fine.

As a young minister I did the same thing most Christians have done in the babyhood stage of their Christianity. I heard people talking about visions and angels, and I prayed something like that would happen to me. It never did.

Then I matured spiritually until I never expected it to happen. I did not pray that it would happen. I did not expect it. But back in 1949 I was praying one day in the last church I pastored. I had shut myself up in the church to wait on God because I had a witness in my spirit that I should do so. Then the Holy Spirit—not my spirit—spoke to me.

Before I tell you what He said, look at this passage of Scripture with me and see how Peter saw a vision and then was led by the Voice of the Spirit of God:

> On the morrow, as they went on their journey, and drew up nigh unto the city, Peter went up upon the housetop to pray about the sixth hour: And he became very hungry, and would have eaten: but while they made ready, he fell into a trance, And saw heaven opened, and a certain vessel descending unto him, as it had been a great sheet knit at the four corners, and let down to the earth:
>
> —Acts 10:9-11

God showed Peter through a vision that He was going to bring in the Gentiles. Now we will skip to the 19th verse:

> While Peter thought on the vision, THE SPIRIT SAID unto him, Behold, three men seek thee. Arise therefore, and get thee down, and go with them, doubting nothing: for I have sent them.
>
> —Acts 10:19,20

These were three men from Cornelius' household. After Peter went there and preached to these Gentiles, he was called on the carpet up in Jerusalem. In the 11th chapter of Acts, Peter is rehearsing the matter there.

> And, behold, immediately there were three men already come unto the house where I was, sent from Caesarea unto me. AND THE SPIRIT BADE ME GO with them, nothing doubting . . . .
>
> —Acts 11:11,12

The Holy Spirit spoke to Peter. It may have been that Peter looked around to see who said that. I don't know. But he knew that the Spirit bade him go.

The Spirit spoke to me as I was waiting there in my church. The Spirit said, "I am going to take you on to revelations and visions."

Immediately, revelations, in line with the Word—I'm not talking about something out of line with the Bible—began to come. Then in 1950 the visions began to come. Eight times Jesus Himself appeared to me and talked to me. There were also other visions.

24

The Spirit Bade Me Go

"Now there were in the church that was at Antioch certain prophets and teachers; as Barnabas, and Simeon that was called Niger, and Lucius of Cyrene, and Manaen, which had been brought up with Herod the tetrarch, and Saul. As they ministered to the Lord, and fasted, THE HOLY GHOST SAID, Separate me Barnabas and Saul for the work whereunto I have called them."

—Acts 13:1,2

The Holy Ghost said. It would be of interest, first of all, to notice under what conditions the Holy Ghost said something. *"As they ministered to the Lord, and fasted, the Holy Ghost said . . . ."*

I am convinced we need to have services where we minister to the Lord. Too often we just minister to one another. Bible studies are good; we need them. Special singing is fine. But too many times we are not singing to the Lord; we are singing to the congregation. Let's have some services where we minister to the Lord. Where we wait on Him. In that kind of an atmosphere the Holy Ghost can speak to us.

This was a group of five ministers. I do not know how the Holy Ghost spoke to them. It could have been that one of the prophets spoke it out. Of this I am sure—they all heard and they all agreed that the Holy Ghost was talking.

The Holy Ghost said, "Separate me Barnabas and Saul for

the work whereunto I have called them . . . . "

Peter said, "The Spirit bade me go . . . . "

After I had been in the ministry many years, death came and fastened itself upon my body. I know when death comes; I have been dead twice and came back. I know how it feels. Actually, I started to fall into the arms of death, when the Spirit of God came on me and lifted me up.

I heard a Voice speak. To me it was audible. I believe it was Jesus. I know that it was the Holy Spirit speaking. We discussed earlier how the Holy Ghost speaks not of Himself, but whatever He hears, that shall He speak. So He heard God or Jesus say it, and He said it.

It sounded like a man's voice. It said, "Thou shalt not die, but thou shalt live. I want you to go teach my people faith. I have taught you faith through my Word. I have permitted you to go through certain experiences. You have learned faith both through my Word and by experience. Now go teach my people what I have taught you. Go teach my people faith."

The moment that voice ceased speaking I was perfectly well.

I have endeavored to be obedient to that heavenly Voice. That is the reason I teach faith so much—I am supposed to do it.

I will refer again now to the time Jesus appeared to me in 1959 in El Paso, Texas. It was during this vision that He told me, "Go teach my people how to be led by my Spirit." I have been dilatory about this. But I am going to do more teaching on this from now on. This is the reason for this book.

25

Guidance Through Prophecy

"Follow after charity, and desire spiritual gifts, but rather that ye may prophesy."   –1 Corinthians 14:1

"Are all apostles? are all prophets? are all teachers? are all workers of miracles?"   –1 Corinthians 12:29

Paul, speaking to the elders of the church at Ephesus in his farewell message said, *"And now, behold, I go bound in the spirit unto Jerusalem, not knowing the things that shall befall me there: Save that the Holy Ghost witnesseth in every city, saying that bonds and afflictions abide me"* (Acts 20:22,23).

Then in the 21st chapter, Paul on his journey landed at Tyre where the ship was to unlade her burden. Luke, the writer of Acts was with Paul. He wrote, *"And finding disciples, we tarried there seven days: who said to Paul through the Spirit, that he should not go up to Jerusalem"* (v. 4).

Paul continued on his journey:

And the next day we that were of Paul's company departed, and came unto Caesarea: and we entered into the house of Philip the evangelist, which was one of the seven; and abode with him. And the same man had four daughters, virgins, which did prophesy. And as we tarried there many days, there came down from Judaea a certain prophet, named Agabus. And when he was come unto us, he took Paul's girdle, and bound his own hands and feet, and said, Thus saith the Holy Ghost, So shall the Jews at Jerusalem bind the man that owneth this girdle, and shall deliver him into the hands of the Gentiles. And when we heard these things, both we, and they of that place, besought him not to go up to Jerusalem. Then Paul answered, What mean ye to weep and to break mine heart? for I am ready not to be bound only, but also to die at Jerusalem for the name of the Lord Jesus. And when he would not be persuaded, we ceased, saying, The will of the Lord be done.

—Acts 21:8-14

Some have thought that Paul missed it. But, when he did go up there and was arrested, Jesus stood by Paul in the night. He appeared to him in a vision. He did not rebuke Paul. He did not tell him that he had missed it. He said, *"Be of good cheer, Paul: for as thou hast testified of me in Jerusalem, so must thou bear witness also at Rome"* (Acts 23:11).

No, Paul did not miss it. What God was doing was preparing Paul for what was ahead of him.

Notice that we have two things here: 1. the gift of prophecy, 2. the ministry of the prophet. They are different. They are not the same. It is a mistake to confuse the two, yet this is often done.

The fact that one prophesies does not make him a prophet. The Word of God plainly teaches that everyone should desire to prophesy (1 Cor. 14:1). If prophesying made you a prophet, then it would seem the Lord said everyone should desire to be a prophet. Yet Paul asked, *"Are all apostles? are all prophets? . . . . "* The answer is no. Since all could not be prophets, God would not tell us to seek something we could not have.

The simple gift of prophecy is speaking unto men to edification and exhortation and comfort (1 Cor. 14:3). Prophecy is a supernatural utterance in a known tongue—your own tongue. (Speaking in tongues is supernatural utterance in an unknown tongue—a tongue unknown to you.) Prophecy can be used in prayer, as well as tongues.

Sometimes when you are prophesying, it seems like there are two of you. It seems to me like I am standing right beside myself. You see, it is coming from my inward man where the Spirit of God who is prophesying abides. I listen with my natural ears to see what He said.

The Office of the Prophet

Now there is the office of the prophet. Without going into detail about it we will touch it briefly concerning guidance. For one to be a prophet, he stands in that office and uses that ministry. Other spiritual gifts besides prophecy must operate in his ministry. The simple gift of prophecy, as we have said, is for speaking unto men for edification, and exhortation, and comfort. In this simple gift of prophecy there is no *foretelling*, no prediction whatsoever. However, in the ministry of the prophet there is foretelling and prediction. He has the revelation gifts (the word of wisdom, the word of knowledge, and/or the discerning of spirits) in operation along with prophecy.

It is important to realize that spiritual things can be misused just as natural things can be misused. Some folks have never realized that. They think that just because it is spiritual it has to be perfect—that it cannot be misused.

I have known people who were at one time wealthy who are now bankrupt because they listened to somebody prophesy how to invest their money.

I remember a dear man who was in my meeting. I knew who he was, but I didn't really know him. I did not know that he would never make a business deal without calling this so-called prophet to prophesy to him what to do.

I said to him, "I seem to be impressed to say this to you. You are going to lose everything you have and go bankrupt if you keep listening to whoever is advising you."

He didn't listen. The poor fellow, who was very wealthy, lost his home and everything he had. I have seen this happen not just one time, but many times.

I have seen ministers who have lost their ministries because of wrong prophecies.

You have to judge prophecies by the Word of God. If it is not in line with the Word of God, it is not right.

Secondly, you have to judge personal prophecies by what you have in your own spirit. If you do not have it in your own spirit, do not accept it.

For years I have travelled extensively in the ministry. Everywhere I go there is always somebody who has a "word" from the Lord for me—sometimes two or three. In all these years only one or two of them have been correct.

Do not build your life on prophecies. Do not guide your life by prophecies. Build your life on the Word! Let those other things be secondary. Put the Word of God first!

People sometimes say, "Well, if God is doing it, it has to be all right."

You have to realize that it isn't exactly God doing it. It is men doing it by the inspiration of the Spirit of God. Anything that man has to do with is not perfect. The Spirit of God is perfect. The gifts of the Spirit in themselves are perfect. But they certainly are not always perfect in manifestation, because they are manifested through imperfect vessels. This is the reason prophecy and tongues with interpretation need to be judged by the Word.

> Let the prophets speak two or three, and let the other judge. If any thing be revealed to another that sitteth by, let the first hold his peace.
>
> —1 Corinthians 14:29,30

"Let the prophets speak . . . ." He is talking about prophets here—not just everybody prophesying. Do not accept it just because a prophet said it. It is to be judged according to the

Bible. We do not judge people. We judge what was said.

Now notice the 30th verse. *"If any thing be revealed to another* (prophet) . . . . " Prophets have revelations. Others might occasionally, but prophets have a ministry along this line.

> And the spirits of the prophets are subject to the prophets.
>
> –1 Corinthians 14:32

Some have said, "God made me do that. I couldn't help but say that." The spirits of the prophets are subject to the prophets. That means you do not *have* to say it. It comes out of your spirit. It is subject to you. The gift of tongues, the interpretation of tongues, and prophecy operate under the unction of the Spirit. And it might be that God through these methods would give us a word of knowledge, a word of wisdom, or revelation as we need it. But we initiate the operation of prophecy. We initiate the operation of tongues and interpretation. We are the ones who have to speak it.

Many times when the Spirit of God is moving, anyone who can prophesy could do so—but that does not mean one should. Also, when the Spirit is in manifestation, anyone who is used in the ministry gift of tongues and interpretation could speak—but that does not mean he should. Have that *unction* of the Spirit to do it—otherwise just sit there and let God move through somebody else who has it.

I held a 7-week meeting in a church years ago. Every single night about the same time, at the same spot in the service, just as they got ready to pass the offering plates, this woman got up and spoke with tongues. She said the same thing in tongues every night. After a while I could have said the same things she said. If nobody else would interpret it, she would. It went out like cold water over the crowd. It deadened the service.

The pastor asked me to teach the auditorium class one

Sunday morning when he had to be out of town. This was unusual—but I finished before the bell rang. One of the deacons said, "Brother Hagin, may I ask a question?"

"Well, yes," I said. I thought it would be in line with the lesson.

He said, "When messages in tongues with interpretation are given in public assembly, shouldn't they be a blessing to the congregation? Should it kill the service?"

That dear woman was sitting right in front of me.

I said, "That is beside the lesson. I hate to get into that right now."

But others, some of the leaders of the church said, "Brother Hagin, we ought to answer that."

So I said, "If it is in the Spirit, it will lift the service high. It will not push it down."

That woman was intelligent enough to catch on to that. She came to me and said, "I am wrong, am I not?"

I said, "Yes ma'am, you are."

She said, "I thought so all the time. There was some witness on the inside of me that knew that. But I wanted to be used of God. I am going to stop that."

I said, "Thank you. You are a real blessing to the church."

Others might have gotten angry about it saying, "They won't allow God to move."

Sometimes folks do speak out, like this woman, without the unction of the Spirit. This does not do away with the fact that her tongues were real. However, they were in imperfect operation. They were misused.

I admonish people to be very careful about personal prophecies. So many lives have been shipwrecked and ruined by not being careful about them. Don't marry someone because somebody prophesied you should. I have seen many such so-called prophecies through the years. I have never seen one of them work out yet. Homes have been broken up by so-called prophecies.

Don't go into the ministry because somebody prophesied you should. Get it on the inside of you for yourself. Then if a prophecy confirms what you already have, that's all right. Jesus said to me when He appeared in that vision in 1959, "If the prophecy confirms what you already have, accept it. If it does not, don't accept it."

The Holy Ghost said, *"Separate me Barnabas and Saul for the work whereunto I have called them"* (Acts 13:2). He had already called them. This was just a confirmation of it.

In the last church I pastored there was a certain young person who was beautiful spiritually. My wife said to me, "I believe the hand of the Lord is on him. God is calling him into the ministry."

I said, "I have that conviction myself. But I am not going to call anybody. I am not going to tell anybody they are called, even if I know they are."

This is why. When one gets out in the ministry it isn't always easy. Paul told the young minister, Timothy, "Endure hardness as a good soldier." When the way gets hard—and it will; you can have the victory, but it will get hard—someone who is not convinced of the call themselves may say, "I just went because Daddy said so." Or, "Somebody prophesied to me. I really don't know that I am called." But one who makes that dedication from his own spirit, who knows God called, will stand through hell or high water.

So I did not say anything to this young person. Then one Sunday night we were all praying around the altar. I went around and laid hands on people to pray as God would lead me. I stopped beside this young man who was kneeling in the altar in intense prayer. I opened my mouth to pray, but I heard these words come out, "This is a confirmation to what I said to you at 3 o'clock in the afternoon as you were praying down in the storm cellar. You asked for a confirmation and this is it. That was Me speaking to you."

After the prayer service I asked, "Were you praying down in the storm cellar at 3 o'clock this afternoon?"

(I wanted to check up—if I am wrong, I want to get right. If I miss it, I just admit, "I missed it." Don't be afraid to say, "I missed it." When I first started learning to drive a car I missed it a few times and ran up over the curb. But I didn't quit driving just because I missed it. Did you? We ought to have as much sense about spiritual things. Just because I missed it, I am not going to quit. I am going to keep going. I will just see to it that I don't miss it again. So I was checking up on it to see.)

This young person said, "Yes, I was praying. You know, Brother Hagin, I have felt for some time that God had a call on my life. I didn't say yes or no. So I was spending time down in the cellar (which was fixed up like a nice basement) praying, meditating, reading the Bible, waiting on God. I felt like the Lord spoke to me and said, 'I have called you to the ministry—and I will confirm it tonight in the service.' But I didn't know how He would."

Remember—if it does not bear witness, or confirm something you already have, do not accept a personal prophecy.

As long as the gift of prophecy stays in the realm of speaking to men for edification, exhortation, and comfort, it is wonderful. Encourage that. But many times someone who prophesies may see a prophet minister with a word of foreknowledge. Then he begins to think, "I prophesy; so I can do that." So he moves out of the place where he should be into the other realm.

A woman came up to me in one of our seminars we held in Tulsa. She had come with a group from a nearby city. She said, "Brother Hagin, this is all new to us. In our town we have a weekly prayer group. I want to ask you something about it. Some of them think I am wrong, but I don't think what we are doing is right. Actually, I don't know if I would call it a prayer meeting—all they ever do is lay hands on one another and prophesy. They spend all afternoon prophesying over one another. And I don't ever get anything but a bad prophecy.

"They prophesied that my mother was going to die within six months. That was eighteen months ago and she is not dead. They prophesied that my husband was going to leave me. He's not saved but he is a fine man and I love him. He is a good provider. We don't have any trouble. Those are just two examples. I always get prophecies that something bad is going to happen—but nothing bad has ever happened."

I said, "No, and it won't either. You are a child of God."

She said, "Isn't that a misuse?"

I said, "Yes, it is."

We need to know these things. It is very easy for babies to be misled and misguided. We can get off track. That's why Paul wrote to the church at Corinth about these things.

26

Guidance Through Visions

"There was a certain man in Caesarea called Cornelius, a centurion of the band called the Italian band, a devout man, and one that feared God with all his house, which gave much alms to the people, and prayed to God alway. He saw in a vision evidently about the ninth hour of the day an angel of God coming in to him, and saying to him . . . . "

–Acts 10:1-3

$\mathcal{S}$ ometimes God leads through visions.

Cornelius was a devout man, but he was not born again. He did not know about Jesus. He was a Jewish proselyte. The angel who appeared to him in this vision could not preach the Gospel to him. God did not call angels to preach the Gospel, but men. The angel did tell him where to send for someone who would preach to him and tell him how to be saved.

Cornelius saw an angel in a vision. Angels also have the ability, as God permits, to take upon themselves a form which can be seen with the natural eye as you see a physical person.

Be not forgetful to entertain strangers: for thereby some have entertained angels unawares.

–Hebrews 13:2

But the Scripture calls Cornelius' experience a vision (Acts 10:3). Therefore, it was a spiritual vision. He saw into the spirit world. And there are angels out there in the spirit world. If anyone else had been present, they would not have seen anything. Yet if the angel had taken on a form visible, anyone could have seen it.

There are three kinds of visions: spiritual visions, trances, and open visions.

In a spiritual vision, you see with the eyes of your spirit—not with your physical eye. When Paul saw the Lord in Acts 9, it was a spiritual vision. He did not see Him with his physical eyes.

> And Saul arose from the earth; and when his eyes were opened, he saw no man: but they led him by the hand, and brought him into Damascus.
>
> —Acts 9:8

When the Lord spoke to him his eyes were shut. Therefore whenever he saw whatever he saw, he was not seeing it with his physical eyes. And when his eyes were opened, he was blind.

The second type of vision is when one falls into a trance. Cornelius did not fall into a trance—but Peter did.

> On the morrow, as they went on their journey, and drew nigh unto the city, Peter went up upon the housetop to pray about the sixth hour: And he became very hungry, and would have eaten: but while they made ready, he fell into a trance, And saw heaven opened, and a certain vessel descending unto him, as it had been a great sheet knit at the four corners, and let down to the earth:
>
> —Acts 10:9-11

When one falls into a trance, his physical senses are suspended. He does not know where he is right at the moment. He is not unconscious, but he does not know what is going on around him. He is more conscious of spiritual things than physical things.

The third type of vision is what I call an open vision. The

vision I have referred to so often in this book which occurred in El Paso in 1959 was an open vision. My eyes were wide open. My physical senses were intact. I did not fall into a trance. Jesus walked into my room. I saw Him with my physical eyes.

Of all the visions I have had, only two were open visions. Three of them occurred when I fell into a trance. The rest were spiritual visions.

There were different types of visions in the Acts of the Apostles. There are different types of visions now.

In visions, sometimes things are symbolic. In Peter's vision they were. He saw all manner of creeping things, both clean and unclean. He had to think on it (Acts 10:19). The Spirit spoke to him as he thought and bade him go with three men to Cornelius' house. He still didn't know exactly what the vision meant. But when he went, things happened, and he began to understand that God had called in the Gentiles as well as the Jews.

> And the angel of the Lord spake unto Philip, saying, Arise, and go toward the south unto the way that goeth down from Jerusalem unto Gaza, which is desert. And he arose and went: and, behold, a man of Ethiopia, an eunuch of great authority under Candace queen of the Ethiopians, who had the charge of all her treasure, and had come to Jerusalem for to worship, Was returning, and sitting in his chariot read Esaias the prophet. Then the Spirit said unto Philip, Go near, and join thyself to this chariot.
>
> —Acts 8:26-29

Some church people admit that God spoke to the apostles such as Peter, but they say that such divine visitations were for the apostles only. Philip was not an apostle. He was elected a deacon first (Acts 6:5). The highest office he ever filled was that of evangelist (Acts 21:8). Isn't it sad that in the church world we have been robbed of the blessings and the supernatural manifestations we should have had because people closed the book on it and said, "That was just for the apostles. All that ceased when the apostles died."

> And there was a certain disciple at Damascus, named Ananias; and to him said the Lord in a vision, Ananias. And he said, Behold, I am here, Lord. And the Lord said unto him, Arise, and go into the street which is called Straight, and inquire in the house of Judas for one called Saul, of Tarsus: for, behold, he prayeth, And hath seen in a vision a man named Ananias coming in, and putting his hand on him, that he might receive his sight.
>
> —Acts 9:10-12

Ananias was not a deacon. He was just a disciple. He was what we would call a layman. Yet the Lord used him. We should all put ourselves into a position where God can use us as He sees fit. We don't have to wait for a vision before we do anything. God may give us a vision, or He may not. An angel may appear, or he may not.

It was a great privilege for me to speak in the church of a great man of God when he was past seventy years of age. He had been filled with the Spirit way back at the turn of the century and had gone out to China as a missionary back in 1912. He told me of many marvelous experiences.

In his church every Friday night they had a Bible study. (I believe he was one of the world's foremost Bible teachers—and I have heard most of them.) He related this to me. He said he would teach certain subjects as the Lord directed, but he also let the congregation suggest subjects by writing them down on a slip of paper. On one occasion, the majority wrote, "We would like some teaching on angels. We have never heard any."

He had spent a number of years teaching in one of the best Pentecostal Bible schools and he thought he could cover the subject in two weeks. But he said, "The more I studied, the bigger it got. I taught six weeks and still did not cover it."

He was an official of his Full Gospel denomination. Soon

after this teaching on angels he was in a business meeting with leaders of that denomination. One matter of discussion concerned the report that some minister of their denomination claimed to have seen an angel. He said that the angel instructed him concerning his ministry. They were about to read him out of the denomination.

He said, "I just sat there and listened. I didn't even comment. I never did talk unless I was called on to talk. I could see the trend. They were about ready to turn him out."

Finally, one brother got up and said, "I believe we ought to hear from Brother S_____. He has been with us from the beginning of the movement. He is one of our most able Bible teachers. Let's hear what he has to say."

He told me he began by telling them about the study of angels he had just completed and taught in his church. Then he said, "I am not the least bit concerned because one of our ministers out of several thousand has seen an angel. The thing that disturbs me is why more of us are not seeing some of them.

"Then secondly," he told them, "if we are going to turn this man out for seeing an angel who instructed him concerning his ministry, what are we going to give our people in the place of it? Do we have anything better? anything more supernatural? anything more scriptural? If we do not, I think we had better stay with what we have."

Quickly, someone jumped to his feet and said, "I move that we table this and forget all about it." They voted unanimously to leave it alone.

In 1963, my office occupied only the den of my little frame home in Garland, Texas. It wasn't really much of an office at that. Some men in another city contacted me. They said, "If you will move your office here, we will set up an office for you. We will buy all the office equipment, hire the secretaries, and pay their salaries. You won't have to pay anything. Let's get some of your material published."

Another man who was an electronic technician said, "Brother Hagin, if you will let me, I will make tapes of all your sermons. It won't cost you a thing. I will furnish all the materials free of charge."

Those offers sounded good. You would think God must be in them. But about that time I was praying with a group. We were having special times of ministering to the Lord. It was the kind of atmosphere Acts 13:1 and 2 speaks of—an atmosphere where God will move.

I was sitting on the platform beside a chair, praying, when suddenly Jesus stood right in front of me. I had my eyes shut. It was a spiritual vision. I did not fall into a trance. Standing right behind Jesus, about two feet to His right and three feet behind Him, was a large angel. I had seen angels before—but never one that big. He must have been 8 feet tall or more.

Jesus talked to me about some things. (And everything He said came to pass.) Occasionally, while He talked, I would glance at that angel. When I did, the angel would open his mouth and start to say something. When I looked back to Jesus, he would not say anything.

After Jesus finished His conversation with me, I asked, "Who is that fellow? What does he represent?"

Jesus said, "That's your angel."

I said, "My angel?"

"Yes," He said, "your angel. You read in the Scriptures that I said concerning the little children that their angel is ever before my Father's face. You don't lose your angel just because you grow up."

(Isn't that comforting! I have that big fellow following me around. Praise the Lord!)

I said, "What does he want?"

Jesus said, "He has a message for you."

Then I got so letter-of-the-Word conscious I could have missed the Spirit. I said, "You are talking to me; why don't You give me the message? Why do I have to listen to an angel? Besides that, the Word of God says as many as are led by the Spirit of God, they are the sons of God. I have the Holy Ghost. Why couldn't the Holy Ghost talk to me?"

Jesus had mercy on me, and patience with me. He said, "Did you ever read in my Word where the angel of the Lord told Philip to go down to the way of Gaza? Wasn't that direction? Wasn't that guidance? Didn't my angel appear to Cornelius, and he wasn't even a born-again man? Didn't the angel tell him what to do? . . . ."

He gave me several more New Testament examples.

Finally, I said, "That's enough. I will listen." Then I looked up to this big fellow and said, "What is it?"

He started this way, "I am sent from the Presence of Almighty God to tell you not to let these men (he called their names) set up an office for you. They have an ulterior motive. They will control your ministry because they will have put in all the money."

Then he called the name of the man who was the radio and electronic technician and said, "Don't let him have any of your tapes. He has an ulterior motive. If he gets them into his hands, he will control them. I am sent from the Presence of Almighty God to tell you that.

"Then I am sent from the Presence of Almighty God to tell you this. The money will come so that you can set up your own office, have your own books, have your own tapes. You will be the head of it, the sole boss, because I am going to tell you what to do, and not some man. Within four months, after everything is paid and cleared out, you will have enough money to get you headed this direction. For I have sent my angels out to cause the money to come."

When the time came, I had $4,000, which was enough to do what the Lord had told me to do. That was the beginning of this ministry.

I could tell more, but this is enough to illustrate that these things do happen. But let me emphasize this—although God does lead us through visions and other supernatural manifestations, I would encourage you NOT to seek a vision. You could get beyond the Word where the devil can deceive you. We often prefer to have a more direct word of guidance, but we don't always have it. So don't try to manufacture it if it is not there. Nowhere does the Bible say that anyone was seeking a vision when it came. They just happened without their seeking it.

Be content, if that is all you ever have, to follow the inward witness. But educate and train and develop your human spirit where that witness becomes real and more real to you.

Then, if God sees fit for supernatural visitations and manifestations, just thank God for them.

Know that the angels of God are with you. Your angel is with you whether you ever see him or not.

27

Listen to Your Heart

"Now when much time was spent, and when sailing was now dangerous, because the fast was now already past, Paul admonished them, And said unto them, Sirs, I perceive that this voyage will be with hurt and much damage, not only of the lading and ship, but also of our lives."
–Acts 27:9,10

Paul did not say, "The Lord told me." He simply said, "I perceive." In his spirit, Paul had an inward perception, an inward premonition, an inward witness. This is the primary way God leads all of us.

Paul did not perceive it *mentally*. He did not have some kind of "vibration." I don't like this vibration business. It is in the psychic realm. You do not find it in the Bible. Paul did not perceive it *physically*. In his *spirit* he had a witness.

That belongs to all of us. The Holy Spirit abiding in our spirits must communicate with us through our spirits—not through our minds. That is why your spirit knows things your head doesn't know. But we have not been taught to listen to our spirits. And sometimes we are reluctant to do so.

The reason that we as Spirit-filled believers continually miss it, make mistakes, and fail is because our spirits which should guide us are kept locked away in prison so to speak. Knowledge, or intellect, has taken the throne.

Any person who shuts his spirit away and never listens to it—because the spirit of man is the candle of the Lord—becomes crippled in life and an easy prey to selfish and designing people.

A very beautiful woman, spiritually—my wife and I had held a meeting for this lady pastor—told me this herself.

An evangelist was coming to town. He got all the churches he could to cooperate with him in a city-wide meeting. He rented the city auditorium. It is a sorry thing to have to say, but everybody in the ministry is not honest. Because this man had a poor credit rating, the city auditorium demanded payment in advance. So he went through this woman pastor. She was gullible enough to say her church would stand responsible for $3000 rent and all newspaper advertising. Crowds of 2000 to 3000 attended every night. He took up a lot of money. But he left town without paying one bill. This woman's church had to take $5000 out of their building fund to cover his expenses.

She told me this about it, "Brother Hagin, if I had listened to my heart, I would never have done that."

I said to her, "I heard you recovered your money."

She said, "I sure did. I found out where he was holding a meeting in another state. I got an airplane ticket and went there. The service had already started. I waited. Just when they were about to turn the service to him I marched down the aisle and toward the platform. An usher tried to stop me. I said, 'No, I am a minister of the Gospel. I want to see this scoundrel.' I walked right up on the platform and plopped myself down beside him.

"I said, 'I have come after my $5000. I will take the offering tonight. I brought my attache case along. We will dump it all in there. And I will stay around here every night until we get it all back.'

"He said, 'Well, now we . . . . '

"I said, 'No, when they say they are going to turn the service over to you, I am going to take the pulpit and tell them what happened. And not only that, I am going to follow you from meeting to meeting. In every meeting I am going to get on the platform and make the announcement.' "

Needless to say, in two nights she had her money and was on her way home. I glory in her spunk.

But the point I want to make is this. She said to me, "Brother Hagin, if I had listened to my spirit. I don't mean a voice. I don't even mean a still, small voice. I just mean the inward witness. I had a check in my spirit. If I had listened to it, I wouldn't have stood good for his debts."

If we as individuals would have listened to our hearts—an inward witness, or an inward voice—we would not have done some things we did.

I have lost money by not listening. I knew on the inside that I should not do it. Why did I do it? Well, why did you do it?

But just because you make a mistake, don't quit. You don't quit physically just because you make a mistake. If the phone rings in the middle of the night and you stumble over a stool and fall down trying to answer it, you don't just lie there. You get up and answer the phone. Just because you bust your shins or stub your toe physically you don't quit. And just because you bust your shins or stub your toe spiritually you don't quit.

As I said, the person who keeps his spirit shut away and never listens to it becomes crippled in life. The person who listens to his spirit is the man or woman, boy or girl who climbs to the top!

If Christians would just check up on the inside of them in most of the affairs of life, they would know what to do.

You do not need to seek guidance when the Bible has already told you what to do. Go ahead and do it. The Bible tells you how to act in every circumstance of life. It tells husbands how to treat wives. It tells wives how to treat husbands. It tells parents how to treat their children. It tells children how to respond to their parents. The Bible tells all of us to walk in love—divine love.

And that divine love, which seeks not its own, is also a matter of the heart.

28

How To Train The Human Spirit

"The spirit of man is the candle of the Lord . . . ." —Proverbs 20:27

The Lord enlightens us and guides us through our spirits. If that be the case—and it is—then we need to become more spirit-conscious. We need to become more conscious of the fact that we are spirit beings, and not just mental or physical beings. We need to train our spirits where they will become safer and safer guides.

One thing which has held back the Christian world as a whole is that we are more physical-conscious (body-conscious) and more mental-conscious (soul-conscious). We have developed the body and the soul, but we have left the spirit of man almost untouched.

I have a cassette teaching tape which has helped many in this area. One young man I know quite well gave his testimony of how it had helped him in one of our recent meetings.

Just a few years ago, when he was 31 or 32, he went into business. He left his salaried job with a total of $5500. He had to use this money for living expenses—he was single at the time—as well as capital. At one point his nest egg dwindled to $50.

He gave this testimony, "I listened to Brother Hagin's tapes. There were three on faith and confession, and one called *How To*

Train The Human Spirit. I went to bed every night listening to that tape. I put it on in the morning and listened to it while I shaved. I listened to it over and over and over again—probably hundreds of times—until that message got into my spirit. Then by listening to my spirit and using my faith, my assets now total in excess of $30 million."

This young man is only about 38 years old now. He is not a preacher. He is a businessman. He has told me how his spirit has spoken to him and told him how to invest and buy land.

I will give the essence of the teaching contained on that cassette in this chapter: How To Train The Human Spirit.

Your spirit can be educated just as your mind can be educated. Your spirit can be built up in strength and trained just as your body can be built and trained. Here are four rules by which you can train and develop your own human spirit.

1. By meditation in the Word
2. By practicing the Word
3. By giving the Word first place
4. By instantly obeying the voice of your spirit

1. BY MEDITATION IN THE WORD OF GOD The most deeply spiritual men and women I know are those who give time to meditation in the Word of God. You cannot develop spiritual wisdom without meditation. God made that fact known to Joshua just after the death of Moses at the very beginning of Joshua's ministry.

> This book of the law shall not depart out of thy mouth; but thou shalt meditate therein day and night, that thou mayest observe to do according to all that is written therein: for then thou shalt make thy way prosperous, and then thou shalt have good success.
>
> —Joshua 1:8

If God did not want Joshua to be prosperous, why did He tell him how to prosper? If He did not want him to succeed, why did

He tell him how to have good success? He wanted Joshua to be successful—and He wants you to be successful.

Paraphrasing this truth in New Testament language, we would say, "The Word of God—particularly the New Testament—shall not depart out of your mouth. But meditate therein day and night, that you may observe to do according to all that is written therein: for then you will make your way prosperous and you will have good success."

If you ever want to do anything great in life, if you ever want to amount to anything in life, *take time to meditate.* Take time to meditate in the Word of God. Start out with at least 10 or 15 minutes a day—then increase the time.

I left the last church I pastored in 1949 and I have been out in the field ministry ever since. I used to do much more fasting and a different kind of praying than I do now. (You learn things as you go along.) Running two services a day—which I always did, and sometimes three—takes a lot out of you physically as well as spiritually. I would teach every morning, pray out loud all afternoon, and preach every night. I ate only one meal a day during my meetings and by putting out so much physical energy, I would grow weak. Then two days a week were my fast days—Tuesday and Thursday. I ate no food and drank no water for 24 hours.

One day the Lord said to me, "I would rather you would live a fasted life instead of having days and periods of fasting."

I said, "What do you mean? I never heard anybody say that?"

He said, "Instead of having certain days you fast and then going back and eating all you want, just live a fasted life. Fasting does not change me anyhow. I am the same before you fast, while you fast, and when you get through fasting. It does not change the Word. It helps you keep your flesh under. So, just don't ever eat all you want. Just keep it under all the time."

Then He said, "Don't spend all that time in the afternoon praying and wearing yourself out before the night service. Lie on the bed and meditate."

So I began to lie there in the afternoons, meditating. And I got further meditating than I ever did praying and fasting. I grew more spiritually.

That is what He is saying in Joshua 1:8. *" . . . for then thou shalt make thy way prosperous . . . . "* I wanted to be prosperous in the ministry. *" . . . and then thou shalt have good success . . . . "* I wanted to have good success in the ministry. This works whether you are in the ministry, whether you raise cattle, or sell automobiles, or whatever you do.

This Word of God shall not depart out of thy mouth. Talk about it. *But thou shalt meditate.* Think on it.

The Hebrew word translated *meditate* also carries this thought with it: *to mutter.* Mutter it. Speak it to yourself.

The Lord led me, before I ever heard anybody teach on meditation, to lie on the bed and mutter the Word. I just said it to myself. And I would have some of the most tremendous services. I developed myself spiritually, and at the same time conserved my physical strength.

I like another translation of Joshua 1:8 which reads like this on the last phrase, *" . . . you shall be able to deal wisely in the affairs of life."* You could not have good success if you did not know how to deal wisely in the affairs of life.

Why would you know how to deal wisely in the affairs of life? Because you meditated in the Word of God and walked in the light of that Word.

2. PRACTICING THE WORD Practicing the Word means being a doer of the Word.

> But be ye doers of the word, and not hearers only . . . .
> —James 1:22

We have many "talkers about the Word," and even many "rejoicers about the Word," but we do not have many "doers of the Word."

Begin to practice being a doer of the Word by doing in all circumstances what the Word tells you to do.

Some have thought that being a doer of the Word meant to keep the Ten Commandments. That is not what James 1:22 means. After all, we under the new covenant have but one commandment—the commandment of love. Jesus said, *"A new commandment I give unto you, That ye love one another; as I have loved you, that ye also love one another"* (John 13:34).

A doer of the Word will do that. If you love someone you won't steal from him. You won't lie about him. The New Testament says that love is the fulfilling of the law. If you walk in love you won't break any law which was given to curb sin.

Being a doer of the Word means that we are to do primarily what is written in the Epistles. They are the letters written to us, the Church. As an example of doing the Word, let us look at some instructions given us in one of the Epistles.

> Be careful for nothing; but in every thing by prayer and supplication with thanksgiving let your requests be made known unto God.
>
> —Philippians 4:6

So do that! Now we don't mind practicing part of this verse—the part that says to pray. But if you practice just that part and not the first part, you are not practicing the Word—you are not a doer of the Word.

The *Amplified* translation of Philippians 4:6 begins, *"Do not fret or have any anxiety about anything . . . ."* First we are told not to fret. If you are going to fret and have anxieties, it will do no good to make requests. That kind of praying does not work. An over-anxious prayer full of fretfulness does not work.

I felt very sorry for a minister who came to me some years ago. But sometimes it doesn't give a man the answer just to sympathize with him. Storms and tests were on in his life. His stomach was upset; he couldn't keep down what he ate. He couldn't sleep. His nerves were shot because of a particular incident.

He came to me for help. I began to tell him what the Word said and how to pray about it. When I encouraged him to take this Scripture and *do it*, he rebelled. He said, "Oh, yes, but everybody doesn't have the faith that you have."

I told him it was not a matter of having a lot of faith, but a matter of endeavoring to practice the Word. I told him if he would practice the Word, his faith would be built up. And I told him how I practice this particular verse.

When I get alone, I read this verse aloud and I tell the Lord that His Word is true and that I believe it.

I told this minister that he would be tempted to say he couldn't help worrying and fretting. But that God had not asked us to do something we cannot do. When God said not to fret— that means we can keep from it. God is a just God and He will not ask us to do something we cannot do.

When I first began practicing this verse it was easy to believe that I could make my requests known unto God—but it was hard to believe that I could *not fret*. However, since God says we don't have to fret, then I would say, "I refuse to fret or have any anxiety about anything."

I tell the Lord that I bring my requests unto Him. Then I thank Him for the answer. This quiets my spirit and pacifies the troubled spirit the devil tries to make me have.

Then I get up and go about my business. Before you know it, however, the devil is trying again to get me. I simply go right back and read this verse again and keep claiming it.

This minister began to practice Philippians 4:6. He told me later that the problem worked out and did not get as big as he was expecting. He was about to be sued over a certain matter, but God helped him out of it.

It is possible to become so fretful over something you cannot eat or sleep. But all you have to do is practice the Word and you will get results.

Philippians 4:7 is a result of practicing Philippians 4:6.

> And the peace of God, which passeth all understanding, shall keep your hearts and minds through Christ Jesus.
>
> —Philippians 4:7

Many people want what this 7th verse talks about—but they don't want to practice what the 6th verse says to do to get it. The *Amplified* translation of the 7th verse says, *"And God's peace . . . which transcends all understanding, shall garrison and mount guard over your hearts and minds in Christ Jesus."* God's peace will keep guard over your heart and your mind.

But can you reap these results and have this peace without being a doer of the Word? No, you really cannot.

The 6th verse tells us not to fret. People who worry and fret, continually think on the wrong side of life. Verse 8 tells us what we are to think about:

> Finally, brethren, whatsoever things are true, whatsoever things are honest, whatsoever things are just, whatsoever things are pure, whatsoever things are lovely, whatsoever things are of good report; if there be any virtue, and if there be any praise, think on these things.
>
> —Philippians 4:8

DO verse 8. *Practice* this verse. Think about the right things. Many people think about the wrong things. You know what they think about because of what they talk about. The Bible says, "out of the abundance of the heart, the mouth speaketh." They continually worry and fret and think on the wrong side of life—and they continually talk unbelief. You cannot be a doer of the Word and continue to talk unbelief. The more you talk about some things, the bigger they get. If something does not meet all of these qualifications—true, honest, just, pure, lovely, of good report—do not think about it and do not talk about it!

The *Amplified* translation of 1 Corinthians 13:7 reads, *"Love . . . is ever ready to believe the best of every person."* I have found through the years that most of the stories I have heard about people do not even meet the first qualification. They are not even true. So don't talk about the stories you hear. Don't even think about them. Some things you hear might even be true—but they might not be pure and lovely, and notice this, and of a good report. Therefore we are not to think about them.

By thinking about such things, we give place to the devil. His greatest weapon is the power of suggestion. He is ever endeavoring to enter your thought life. That is why we are told in God's Word to, " . . . *think on these things.*"

In the Epistles, particularly, God the Holy Spirit is speaking to the Church. So meditate on these letters and what He has to say—and be a doer of the Word. You will grow spiritually.

3. GIVE THE WORD FIRST PLACE The training, the developing, the educating of our spirits comes by giving the Word of God first place in our lives.

> My son, attend to my words; incline thine ear unto my sayings.
> Let them not depart from thine eyes; keep them in the midst of thine heart.
> For they are life unto those that find them, and health to all their flesh.
> —Proverbs 4:20-22

God says in this passage, "*Attend to my words* (Give heed to them—Put them first): *incline thine ear unto my sayings* (Listen to what I have to say); *Let them not depart from thine eyes* (Keep looking at the Word of God); *keep them* (my Words) *in your heart.*"

There are rich dividends for doing this. Why is it that God tells us to put His Words first, and to listen to what He has to say, to keep looking at His Word, and to keep His Word in our heart? It is because " . . . *they* (His Words) *are LIFE unto those that find them, and HEALTH to all their flesh.*"

The margin of the King James says the word translated *health* is the Hebrew word for *medicine*. His Words are, "medicine to all their flesh." There is healing in the Word.

In the twelve years I pastored there were members who would get sick, go to the hospital, and afterward ask for prayer. I am not saying that it is wrong to have a doctor, certainly not. We believe in hospitals and doctors. Thank God for them. But I am saying, why not put God's Word first. Sometimes as a last resort, Christians will turn to the Word.

A Baptist minister, who didn't even particularly believe in divine healing at the time, told of how he'd had problems with his tonsils. His doctor kept insisting that they be removed. So the date was set.

It was his family's custom to read the Bible and pray together each morning before the children went to school. On the very date he was scheduled to enter the hospital, their Scripture passage was the one which tells of King Asa, who got a disease in his feet and instead of seeking the Lord, he sought unto physicians and he died (2 Chron. 16:12).

The minister said he was struck by this. He realized that he had not even prayed about his tonsils. He shared this with his wife and children and asked that they pray together about his tonsils.

When they prayed, the Lord told him not to have them removed. To his astonishment, the Lord healed the tonsils and he has had no more trouble with them.

There is a lesson to be learned here. The Bible does not imply that King Asa died because he put the physicians first. However, it does imply that he should have put the Lord first. We should train ourselves to put the Lord first.

We should train ourselves to ask ourselves concerning any matter, "What does God's Word have to say about this?" We should ask ourselves what God has to say about anything that may come up in our life—and then put that Word first.

Sometimes family and friends will try to rush you into things—but you need to think about what the Word of God says.

Put God's Word first in every area of life.

4. INSTANTLY OBEY THE VOICE OF YOUR SPIRIT

The human spirit has a voice. We call that voice *conscience*. Sometimes we call it *intuition*, an *inner voice*, or *guidance*. The world calls it a *hunch*. But what it is, is your spirit speaking to you. Every man's spirit, saved or unsaved, has a voice.

The human spirit, as we have seen in previous chapters, is a spiritual man, a spirit man, an inward hidden man. He is hidden to the physical senses. You cannot see him with the physical eyes, nor touch him with your physical hands. This is the man who has become a new creature in Christ (2 Cor. 5:17). When a man is born again, his spirit becomes a new spirit.

God prophesied through both Ezekiel and Jeremiah that a time would come when He would take the old stony heart out of men and put in a new one. He said that He would put His Spirit into us. Under the New Covenant, this new birth became available.

The new birth is a rebirth of the human spirit. As 2 Corinthians 5:17 tells us, if any man be in Christ, he is a new creature—everything that was old in his spirit, the old nature, is taken away, and all things have become new.

As you give this newborn spirit the privilege of meditating on the Word of God, this becomes the source of its information. Your spirit will become strong and the inward voice of your conscience, educated in the spirit, will become a true guide.

Did you notice that meditation in the Word, practicing the Word, giving the Word first place, all come before obeying your spirit? You see, if your spirit has had the privilege of meditating in the Word, of practicing the Word, of putting the Word first— then your spirit is an authoritative guide.

"The spirit of man is the candle of the Lord . . . . " Your newborn spirit has within it the Life and Nature of God. The Holy Spirit dwells within your spirit. *" . . . Greater is he that is in you, than he that is in the world"* (1 John 4:4). The Holy Spirit

dwells in your spirit. God has to communicate with you through your spirit because that is where He is. Your spirit gets its information through Him.

Learn to obey the voice of your spirit.

If you are not accustomed to doing that, of course, you will not get there quickly. As we have said, your spirit can be built up and strengthened as your body can be built and strengthened. Your spirit can be educated as your mind can be educated. But just as you did not begin school in the first grade one week and graduate from the twelfth grade the next week, your spirit will not be educated and trained overnight.

If you will follow these four points and practice them, however, after a while you can know the will of God the Father even in the minor details of life. You will receive guidance and will always instantly get either a *yes* or a *no*. You will know in your spirit what you should do.

29

Praying With the Spirit

"For if I pray in an unknown tongue, my spirit prayeth, but my understanding is unfruitful. What is it then? I will pray with the spirit, and I will pray with the understanding also: I will sing with the spirit, and I will sing with the understanding also."

— 1 Corinthians 14:14-15

One of the greatest spiritual exercises there is, is to pray in tongues every single day. Your spirit then is in direct contact with the Father of spirits.

> For he that speaketh in an unknown tongue speaketh not unto men, but unto God: for no man understandeth him; howbeit in the spirit he speaketh mysteries.
>
> — 1 Corinthians 14:2

It is your spirit praying when you pray in tongues—the Holy Ghost gives the utterance, but it is your spirit praying. Paul said, *"For if I pray in an unknown tongue, my spirit prayeth . . . ."*

I have always followed the policy of doing a lot of praying in tongues daily. It keeps my spirit in contact with the Father of spirits. It helps me become more spirit-conscious.

When you pray in tongues, your mind grows quiet—because you are not praying out of your mind. And once your mind is

139

quiet, you become more conscious of your own spirit, and of spiritual things.

Get out of the sense realm. Get out of the flesh realm. Get out of the human reasoning realm.

Get over into the faith realm and into the spirit realm. Faith is of the spirit—*and that's where the great things happen!*